LEADER✔ANTAGE
7 ESSENTIAL STEPS TO PEAK LEADERSHIP

Lead to your peak!

*Prisafle
Archangel
8/3/22*

LEADER**V**ANTAGE

7 ESSENTIAL STEPS TO PEAK LEADERSHIP

Priscilla Archangel, Ph.D.

Papilion Publishing

Editing: Ilene Stankiewicz
Cover design and illustrations: Melanie Dunn
Layout: Melanie Dunn and Sean Graham

Printed in the United States of America
First Printing

Publisher's Cataloging-In-Publication Data
Names: Archangel, Priscilla, author.
Title: LeaderVantage : 7 essential steps to peak leadership / Priscilla
    Archangel, Ph.D.
Description: Plymouth, MI : Papilion Publishing, [2021]
Identifiers: ISBN 9781734897302 (softcover) | ISBN 9781734897319 (Kindle-
    MOBI) | ISBN 9781734897326 (Nook-EPUB)
Subjects: LCSH: Leadership--Handbooks, manuals, etc. | Executive ability--
    Handbooks, manuals, etc. | Management--Handbooks, manuals, etc.
Classification: LCC HD57.7 .A734 2021 (print) | LCC HD57.7 (ebook) | DDC
    658.4092--dc23

                    ISBN: 978-1-7348973-0-2 (softcover)
                    ISBN: 978-1-7348973-1-9 (Kindle - MOBI)
                    ISBN: 978-1-7348973-2-6 (Nook - EPUB)

*This book is dedicated to all the leaders
I've worked with over the past 35 years
who have taught me priceless lessons on leadership,
and whose examples have motivated me to learn and grow.
You are the wind beneath my wings.*

CONTENTS

ACKNOWLEDGMENTS

M y inspiration for all the topics in this book come from my wonderful clients, colleagues, and friends, along with the many *nonfiction* business challenges about which I've read. I have observed, experienced, coached, and consulted with others through these situations in a variety of ways, and hope you will "see yourself" in the examples throughout the book. Not because I purposely wrote about a specific person, rest assured that I didn't. But instead, because many of us experience these similar situations and we can all learn from one another.

Most of all, I want to thank God for His wisdom as I continue on this journey; my husband, Peter, for his unending support and encouragement; and the rest of my "tribe"—my mother, Peggy Thompson, my sister, Susan McCloud, my long time colleagues Victoria Jones and Debra Walton, and my partner in prayer, LaTonya Jackson.

And finally, thank you to Ilene Stankiewicz of Beyond Words Business Communications for meticulously editing this work for me, Melanie Dunn and Sean Graham for providing graphic design, and Linda Kleist at Identity Creative for providing bursts of creativity.

PREFACE

My passion for leadership began over three decades ago. At that time, I was starting my career as a Human Resources professional in a Fortune 10 company, and I observed leaders exhibiting a variety of capabilities and behaviors in diverse settings. Because of my role, I had a close-up view of how their team members, colleagues, and senior leaders interacted with them. I learned about their strengths and developmental needs. I observed their insecurities and passion points. Some were effective in their leadership styles while others were not so effective. Certain leaders could "get away" with behaviors that would be deemed inappropriate for others. Some leaders could get results from their teams with seemingly little effort while other leaders had to work hard to build productive relationships. So I've seen the benefits of good leaders who bring out the best in individuals, teams, and organizations. And I've seen the negative impact of toxic leaders who crush the energy of their teams.

Having studied psychology as an undergrad, I had a fascination with understanding behavior and motivation. My natural proclivity was to help these leaders grow and develop, but first I needed to make sure I understood good leadership. That's when I decided to go back to school to really study the topic, and I applied for a Ph.D. program in Human and Organizational Systems. Since then, I have spent decades learning more about leadership and becoming a better leader myself. I've also shared my insights with others through coaching executives; consulting on organizational strategies, development and design; facilitating learning experiences; and speaking and writing. My greatest joy is seeing the light in others' eyes as they grasp a concept, gain a new insight, understand a more effective leadership style, and most notably, improve their leadership effectiveness.

I've had the opportunity to:

1

✓ Lead global human resources teams
✓ Direct multiple rounds of workforce restructuring and reductions
✓ Recruit and staff new leadership teams
✓ Shape and integrate differing cultures
✓ Design and develop organizations
✓ Deal with every imaginable and unimaginable performance and behavioral issue
✓ Assess, train, and coach leaders

I've collaborated with and observed business and leadership challenges in a variety of organizations and industries. And particularly over the past six years, I have written about my resulting insights. This book is a compilation of those writings, organized into seven strategic areas, which reflect several basic beliefs.

The *first* is that every person is created with a unique set of skills and passions. And each of us exists for a purpose that we should live our lives to understand and fulfill. As we join various teams and organizations over the course of our lives, we must ensure that we are aligning our skills, interests, and purpose with a group of people where it can flourish, and that we can complement one another. A leader's function is to provide influence, strategy, and structure to accomplish collective goals and objectives.

The *second* belief is that it is our responsibility to take advantage of the opportunities we have to lead others well. Leaders show up in obvious places, distinguished by lofty titles and hefty compensation packages. They also show up in everyday places—coaching kids' sports teams, as a barista at your local coffee shop, or greeting visitors at your front desk. Leaders are identified by the influence they exercise, encouraging others to pursue a goal. As my friend John Maxwell says in his book, *The Five Levels of Leadership*, sometimes their influence emanates from their position, where others follow them because they should. But people follow the *best* leaders because of who they *are* and what they *represent*.

The *third* belief is we all must be lifelong learning leaders. While some people naturally possess good leadership qualities, more often the rest of us must *learn* over time how to increase our leadership effectiveness. Good leadership capabilities are a result of nature and nurture; the preferences and styles we're born with, and the learning and experiences we gain over time. As we apply ourselves to the effective study of good leadership, we become equipped to assume greater leadership responsibilities to accomplish even greater goals.

Each article in this book highlights typical issues faced by leaders and provides practical steps you can use to address them. The articles are designed to challenge you to have greater self-awareness, along with professional growth and development that will produce better results for your team and organization.

My hope is that by reading this book, you will find tangible insights to grow your leadership capabilities and equip you for leadership success.

INTRODUCTION

Jeb came home exhausted at the end of the work week. But it wasn't just this week. He felt the same way every week. Regarded as one of the smartest leaders in the organization, Jeb was working hard on several major projects which would bring tremendous revenue to his business unit, and he was on the short list for promotion to vp within the next two years at his company. This was the big leap he had been waiting for. Yet somehow, the leadership approach Jeb used during the first 20 years of his career wasn't working like it had in the past. Three months into a new assignment, he was beginning to experience greater difficulty in motivating and aligning his team's individual interests with corporate goals, getting them to bring new ideas forward, and collaborating with peers in other business units. Left unaddressed, his results would be negatively impacted. So Jeb knew he needed to change his approach to leadership quickly, but he wasn't sure what to do.

Jeb decided to call Sue, his former mentor, who had retired from her evp role at the company several years earlier. He had spoken with her four or five times since she left. Jeb worked for Sue when he first joined the company 15 years ago, and she knew his style as well as the corporate culture. Sue was known to be very perceptive and organizationally savvy, and she had a track record of developing strong leaders. Sometimes her insights made Jeb wince, but he was desperate and needed to talk with someone who could help him. Sue chuckled when she answered the phone. She was still well connected within the organization and wasn't surprised to see his name on her caller ID. Surprisingly, she was available for breakfast the next morning and Jeb jumped at the chance to sit down with her.

Sue greeted Jeb warmly when they met at an out-of-the-way breakfast spot 14 hours later. He didn't want to run into colleagues at one of the more popular restaurants and have people guessing as to the reason for their meeting. After quickly placing their orders, Jeb jumped right into the reason for their meeting. He described the challenges he was facing, the approach he was using to lead his team and interact with others, and the results he was getting. Sue listened intently, asked questions occasionally, and then smiled. Jeb paused for a moment, wondering what she was thinking. Then she made one simple statement: "If you want to *transition* to the next level of leadership, you need to *transform* your leadership." Jeb's disappointment was visible. He was expecting her to dissect organizational problems, not his leadership. What did she mean?

Sue let Jeb sit with his frustration for a moment. She had observed his leadership style and skills for many years, first when he was a member of her team and then as he rotated to other positions within the organization. She participated in leadership team discussions where his performance and potential were reviewed. She knew his capabilities as well as his shortcomings. Sue also knew the leadership style necessary to be effective in Jeb's current and future roles at the company. And she knew the moment would come when he would *sincerely* ask her what he needed to do to transition to the next level.

The conversation wasn't new. But maybe Jeb was finally committed to transforming his style. In the past, he continually made excuses to justify his own approach. He "didn't think it took all of that to be successful as a leader." Jeb wanted to be true to himself and not try to act like someone else. He had always gotten ahead because of his technical understanding of the product and his ability to predict the future direction of the market. But lately, more people were questioning his emotional intelligence. He had completed a number of in-house leadership development courses, even met with a coach a few times, but he tended to resist changing. His best friend and colleague, Barry, teased him about being stubborn.

Sue kept in touch with Jeb even after she retired because she saw his potential and hoped one day they would be able to have the conversation they were now having. In fact, she even planned for it. Before she left the house that morning, she slipped an object into her pocket anticipating this was the right time to pull it out. Thankfully, it was. She pulled out a toy Camaro vehicle and set it on the table between them. Jeb was momentarily speechless. He wasn't sure where

Sue was coming from. Sue quickly spoke up and explained the car was her grandson's toy. He plays with it whenever he comes to visit her. He starts out by running it all around the floor, creating a story in his six-year-old mind. Then he picks it up, starts twisting the pieces, and voila! It becomes a superpower called a Transformer, overcoming all evil in his imaginary story. But the beauty of it is whether it looks like a Camaro or a Transformer, both use the same components. In fact, even when it looks like a Camaro, it's still called a Transformer. Yet it's capable of accomplishing far more in its Transformer mode.

Sue and Jeb were finished eating and Sue invited Jeb to walk across the street to a nearby park. It was a bright, sunny summer morning, and it wasn't long before they saw butterflies alighting on the various flowers. Sue stopped and pointed them out. Then she asked Jeb what he knew about the growth of a butterfly. A bit confused, he quickly recalled they start out as a caterpillar, then go into a cocoon, and finally emerge as a butterfly. "That's right," said Sue. "But did you know that butterflies go through four stages—egg, larva, pupa, and adult? Each stage has a different goal. And at every stage it's still a butterfly, even though it doesn't look like one."

Jeb was beginning to understand. Both the Transformer toy and the butterfly start out looking different from their final state, less effective, with untapped capabilities. In order to reach their full potential, they must undergo change. The process of change leverages their existing strengths in new and different ways. They become stronger and are able to really fulfill the purpose for which they were created. Anything else is falling short of the reason for their existence.

As he sat through a variety of company sponsored leadership classes over the years, Jeb always felt like someone was trying to change him from the person he truly was. He resisted some of the learnings shared during those times in order to be "true to himself"; it felt odd to model behavior to which he wasn't accustomed. Now he understood it wasn't about becoming someone he wasn't. It was about understanding, leveraging, and applying his strengths with a different emphasis to gain better results. His intellect, personality, and passions were still the same. But he needed to recognize how to use them to improve his relationships with coworkers, manage organizational politics, and understand the business environment around him.

Jeb mentally kicked himself for being so thick-headed. Sue smiled and told him how long she had been waiting for this moment—for him to realize the need for transforming his leadership approach. She had broached the subject many times over the years, but to no avail. Sue recognized Jeb had to be ready. He had to hit his head against the proverbial brick wall long enough until he became committed to the need to change from within; it couldn't come as pressure from someone else.

Sue was gracious in never giving up on Jeb. She reminded him there were four key elements to think about regarding his transformation.

1. **Authenticity**

   This isn't about becoming like someone else. This is about understanding the most effective qualities of leadership and connecting them with his own strengths.

2. **Motivation**

   Change doesn't occur without reaching a tipping point of readiness. This occurred when Jeb finally recognized the current state was no longer viable and envisioned the future in a way to pull him forward.

3. **Visibility**

   Transformation starts on the inside, usually with a shift in values. But it is accompanied by a visible change in behavior or appearance recognized by others.

4. **Results**

   True transformation is followed by manifesting a different outcome.

Jeb was all in now. He was committed to transformation and understood the need. Though nothing had happened yet, his spirit felt lighter because he had a better vision of the future. And Sue's confidence in his ability to transition to the next level was encouraging.

Their two hours together had flown quickly, and Sue had to get to another meeting. "But wait," said Jeb, "where and how do I start? Do I pull out all the leadership material I've accumulated on my bookshelves and just start reading it?" Sue smiled. "That's a good start," she said. "Meet me next Saturday morning and I'll share with you the seven essential steps I've found to be helpful in this process."

Jeb drove home contemplating his future. The challenges with many of his projects were still there, but he felt he had a path forward to become a stronger leader, with increased effectiveness in the organization.

When he arrived at his office on Monday morning, the first thing he did was to pull out the materials from corporate leadership trainings he had participated in over the past several years. In particular, he sat down and studied a leadership profile from an assessment he took six months ago. Frankly, he hadn't spent as much time with it as he should have. Yet now as he read through it, he became more aware of how his attitude and approach impacted the results within the organization. He looked forward anxiously to his next meeting with Sue, wondering what she would share with him.

Jeb arrived early the following Saturday morning and was sipping his coffee when Sue sat down and gave him a sheet of paper with seven words on it: *purpose, perspective, values, traits, behaviors, tools, and ideas.* He read them quickly, then looked to her with interest. After they ordered breakfast, she told him her most significant accomplishment during her 40-year career was to be able to look back at the leaders she developed along the way. Coming from someone with her technical accomplishments, numerous patents, and industry awards, this surprised Jeb.

Sue continued by sharing that over the years, she identified seven essential steps that provide a vantage point for leaders to be more effective in their roles and gain improved results with their teams. She recognized that by virtue of their position and responsibilities, leaders always have a better view than others in the organization, they understand the broader impact of decisions and behaviors, and they influence outcomes at more levels of the organization. These essential steps help leaders to positively impact their leadership results and reach their peak effectiveness.

Sue went on to explain the meaning of each step.

1. **Purpose**

   Leadership **Purpose** is the *why* behind an individual's leadership. Leaders must have clarity as to why they are in their roles, what they are passionate about accomplishing, how their leadership will make a difference, and why they are called to the work. Purpose transcends the organization or environment where a leader may apply their capabilities.

2. **Perspective**

   Leadership **Perspective** is the foundational viewpoint that helps guide leaders' decisions. It drives how they think about and approach work and relate to colleagues.

3. **Values**

   Leadership **Values** are the principles and standards that support constructive leadership. They are a leader's foundational beliefs about what is important as a leader leads.

4. **Traits**

   Leadership **Traits** are the distinguishing characteristics of successful leaders. Many traits are rooted in gaining the emotional intelligence to have self-awareness of how the leader is perceived by others, and to successfully relate to others to accomplish organizational goals.

5. **Behaviors**

   Leadership **Behaviors** are the actions and attitudes supporting constructive leadership. Behaviors are the outward manifestation of values. It's what leaders *do* on a daily basis.

6. **Tools**

   Leadership **Tools** are the most essential techniques, tips, and strategies that equip leaders to enhance leadership effectiveness.

7. **Ideas**

   Leadership **Ideas** are the basis for pursuing goals, particularly those that may be beyond our current capabilities, yet are fueled by our passions. Leaders drive these concepts forward, but it's important to have a realistic assessment of the context to optimize their chances for success.

Sue's decades of experience led her to the conclusion that as a collective, these concepts form the keys to equip leaders for success. In her last few years with the company, she began to gather a number of articles that helped explain each concept better. She offered to send Jeb a group of articles on each topic every few weeks so that he could read and learn from them. In particular, she told him they would offer practical steps he could use to apply his learnings. Jeb jumped at the chance to continue to absorb Sue's wisdom. He was becoming more aware of his need for development and knew she would guide him well in the process.

Jeb went home energized, waiting for Sue's email with articles on the first topic, Leadership **Purpose**.

Step 1.

The "why" behind
your leadership

L eadership **Purpose** is the why behind your leadership. It transcends the organization or environment where a leader may
apply his or her capabilities. Leaders must have clarity on why they
are in their roles, what they are passionate about accomplishing, how
their leadership will make a difference, and why they are called to
the work. For many leaders, this is an evolutionary process. As they
gain experience in their leadership roles and life, they also become
more aware of where they add the most value to others and where
their passions lie. This vantage point enables them to have a laserlike
focus on those activities that will be most productive in accomplishing their goals.

These articles that are part of Step 1 should make you stop and
reflect on why you're doing some of the things you're doing. They will
require you to pause and think, probably for longer than you expect,
instead of just moving quickly forward. You want to be very sure that
your unique skills, abilities, and passions are being applied in the right
space to align with your purpose. I hope you'll be challenged, and you
may find that you need to make some changes in the direction of your
work. This won't always be comfortable, but you will perform at your
best when your work aligns with your purpose.

Take your time and read just one article each day. This will
give you the opportunity to contemplate what you've read.

1. DISCOVERING YOUR LEADERSHIP PURPOSE
Being the Best You

"If a man is called to be a street sweeper, he should sweep streets even as Michelangelo painted, or Beethoven composed music, or Shakespeare wrote poetry. He should sweep streets so well that all the hosts of heaven and earth will pause to say, 'here lived a great street sweeper who did his job well.' "

—MARTIN LUTHER KING, JR., CIVIL RIGHTS LEADER

We frequently talk about purpose in the context of individuals or organizations, but there are other areas where the identification and understanding of purpose is critical. One such instance is in the context of leadership. Isadore Sharp, founder and chairman of the iconic Four Seasons Hotel brand, provides a great example.

Sharp finished college and earned an architecture degree before he joined his father's construction business in the Toronto area. After building several motor hotels, he recognized that his passion lay not in constructing and owning hotel buildings, but in providing a premier guest experience and level of customer service. His desire was to "welcome customers and treat them like guests coming into our home."[1] So Sharp shifted from being a hotel owner-operator to managing hotel properties. His priority was a commitment to the Golden Rule, where employees and guests alike were treated with respect. Along the way, he had to examine the behavior of his senior leadership team and part company with those who couldn't lead by example. As a result, with over 100 properties in over 40 countries and annual revenues in excess of $4 billion, both customer and employee retention are high. And for 22 consecutive years, the company has been on the list of 100 Best Places to Work.

Sharp understood that his leadership purpose was to provide a premier level of hospitality and service. And over time, he recognized the importance of building the right team around him—a team whose performance aligned with that purpose. Today he fulfills his purpose based on the leadership strengths of treating guests with respect and sincerity, and providing the right location and environment for a first-class stay. He consistently embeds that philosophy into every aspect of his organization's processes, rewards, and behaviors, and believes a true leader influences not from a position of power, but from a position of respect.[2] Sharp's leadership purpose and strengths then work together to accomplish his leadership goal of generating a reasonable profit that benefits the company, hotel owners, customers, and employees.

Leadership purpose forms the "why" of your leadership. Are you seeking a leadership role simply because of the power, position, people, or profits? Or are you leading because of the purpose, mission, and vision you are pursuing, no matter the size of the role? *Leadership strengths* are the capabilities and critical success factors necessary to operate in your purpose. And *leadership goals* are the results you accomplish in your work.

Great Leaders Have Great Leadership Purpose

Leaders are most successful when they lead based on a deep sense of purpose. This passion provides a level of inner drive that enables them to envision more, attempt more, and achieve more. *Fortune's* annual list of The World's 50 Greatest Leaders[3] includes individuals who lead based on their purpose. Here are a few examples:

Stephen Curry, point guard for the Golden State Warriors
Curry is described as arrogant on the court and humble off the court. "I know why I play the game, and it's not to score 30 points a night, but it's to use the stage I'm on. I've been put here for a specific purpose: to be a witness and to share my testimony as I go through it."[4] So Curry uses his leadership strength of playing basketball to accomplish his leadership goal of winning, and fulfills what he sees as his ultimate leadership purpose—sharing his testimony.

Bono, lead singer of U2 and cofounder of One
Most people know and respect Bono as a music legend. But Bono's real legacy is his leadership purpose of leveraging his stardom to convince others to be leaders of change. He does this by utilizing his leadership strength of raising money through his One campaign. His leadership goal is to improve the conditions of people in impoverished nations by eliminating debt and providing health care and electricity, among other initiatives.

Bill and Melinda Gates, cochairs and trustees, Bill and Melinda Gates Foundation
A formidable team, Bill shifted from leading Microsoft, the company he founded, to invest billions in their foundation. Their leadership purpose is to reduce inequity by solving world problems, because they believe that all lives have value. Bill leverages his leadership strength of candidly confronting world leaders about the fundamental problems impacting people in their respective nations and providing investments to address them. Melinda has the ability to connect with everyone she meets, especially those experiencing the worst social stigmas. Their leadership goal is addressing four key global problems: health; development; growth and opportunity; and policy and advocacy. Over the past 20 years, hundreds of millions of people have been positively impacted by their efforts. Warren Buffett—friend, fellow trustee, and billionaire—who has also invested his money in their foundation, says that "Every one of their actions has a multiplier effect. They act with a unity of purpose."[5]

From Purpose to Strengths to Goals

These individuals have led with *purpose*, leveraging their *strengths* to achieve a *goal*. When you learn their stories, you realize they didn't choose their own leadership purpose. Their leadership purpose chose them through a confluence of life experiences, natural inclinations, and innate forces that gave meaning to their daily existence. Their leadership strengths became clear based on their capabilities. And their leadership goals were reflected in their results.

Each of us has the potential to be a great leader, once we answer the key questions of:

- **Why do you want to lead?**
  This is your purpose, which encompasses your mission and vision.

- **How will you get it done?**
  These are your strengths, based on your capabilities.

- **What do you want to accomplish?**
  This is your goal, which will be seen in your results.

But you don't have to be famous to be a great leader. You only have to discover your leadership purpose and work to fulfill it. You only have to impact the people and situations assigned to you in your sphere of influence. You only have to be the best YOU.

1. Diane Eng, "How the Founder of the Four Seasons Stumbled into the Hotel Business," *Fortune*, March 29, 2016, http://fortune.com/2016/03/29/four-seasons-hotels-isadore-sharp/.

2. Micah Solomon, "Four Seasons Leader Isadore Sharp Treats Employees Right So They Treat Customers Right," *Forbes*, August 17, 2015, https://www.forbes.com/sites/micahsolomon/2015/08/17/four-seasons-leader-isadore-sharp-treat-employees-right-so-they-treat-customers-right/#48e51c533031.

3. Geoff Colvin, "The World's 50 Greatest Leaders," *Fortune*, March 24, 2016, http://fortune.com/2016/03/24/worlds-greatest-leaders-2016-intro/.

4. Charles Chandler, "Stephen Curry: 'I Can Do All Things through Christ,' " Billy Graham Evangelistic Association, April 19, 2016, http://billygraham. org/story/stephen-curry-i-can-do-all-things-through-christ/.

5. Geoff Colvin, "The World's 50 Greatest Leaders," *Fortune*, March 24, 2016, http://fortune.com/2016/03/24/worlds-greatest-leaders-2016-intro/.

2. PIVOT TO PURPOSE
Moving from a Career to a Calling

"The meaning of life is to find your gift.
The purpose of life is to give it away."

—PABLO PICASSO, SPANISH PAINTER, SCULPTOR, PRINTMAKER, CERAMICIST, STAGE DESIGNER, POET, AND PLAYWRIGHT

What were you doing as a teenager that really excited you, and that you continue to do today? A speaker posed this question years ago while presenting to a group on the topic of understanding your strengths and passions in life. Several years later, when I was at a pivotal point in my career—trying to decide whether to take the "safe" route, which required less faith, or take the "risky" route, which required a lot of faith—it helped me make my decision. I recognized four key things I did during my teens that I was passionate about, and I continued with these themes later in life.

Writing
When I was about 14, with no prodding from my parents I decided to read 1 Corinthians in the Bible and write down, chapter by chapter, what it meant to me. I analyzed and tried to understand these chapters

and relate them to current life. Thirty years later, I continued that theme by writing a book of insights reflecting a faith-based approach to leadership. And I've followed that by writing a monthly blog for individuals, teams, and organizations focused on developing successful leadership skills. For me, the creativity of writing is intellectually stimulating, and I realize it's a passion I must pursue in my life.

Speaking

When I was a senior in high school, my aunt encouraged me to enter the Michigan Junior Miss Pageant. As I completed the application process, I had to decide what I would do for the "talent" portion of the competition. Traditionally, contestants sing, dance, or play an instrument. I knew I didn't sing or dance well enough for such an event. Though I had taken piano lessons for years, I wasn't really good at it. Instead, I decided to give a dramatic reading. The drama teacher from my high school coached me, and I received a standing ovation! I realize now that I get an emotional rush when I'm on a platform in front of an audience and I have a powerful message to deliver. I focus on connecting with members of the audience and am excited to positively impact their lives.

Processes and Organization

All through high school, after classes, I worked in the office of a small company doing clerical work. I became very knowledgeable about the processes and assumed a lot of responsibility within the team. During my college years, I became the business manager of a singing group, handling bookings, travel arrangements, and the administrative duties. Again, I enjoyed organizing their work and thinking through the processes, and I calmly handled the pressure and demands of the various roles. During this time, I gained an initial appreciation for well thought out approaches to business, a skill set I continued to develop during three decades in corporate America, and I continue to rely upon in my business today.

Consulting and Coaching

In college, I initially wanted to be a therapist, until I realized I wasn't gifted in dealing with more acute mental and emotional issues. Instead, I recognized the consulting and coaching opportunities within human resources/organizational development. I was able to support leaders and teams of all sizes in their growth and development, and leverage my process focus. I also gained valuable observations regarding organizational behavior that became the foundation for my passion around leadership.

Career versus Calling

Once I recognized these areas of passion, I knew I had to take the "risky" route, the leap of faith. My 30-year *career* became a valuable stepping-stone, where I had developed these skills in a particular context. Now it was time to pivot and make it the primary focus of my work: I was moving into my *calling!*

You may be wondering whether you are working in your *career* or your *calling*. Well, simply put, if you're working for recognition and compensation, you have a career. If you're working for something bigger than yourself, and accomplishing more than you imagined, you have a calling. A calling is work you "can't not" perform. It's work that comes with great passion and excitement, where you don't count the hours, and you are not *primarily* driven by income.

Finding You

So how do you find your calling? Begin by answering these questions:

1. **What were your themes during your teen years?**
   Identify them. What problems did you naturally solve? What did you spend time doing that no one had to make you do?

2. **What things do you do that add value and generate compliments from others?**
   These are typically your strengths. What is it about how you do

them that generates positive feedback? In the roles you're in today, how do your strengths compliment your responsibilities?

3. **What is your biggest dream?**
    Write it down, even if you can't figure out how to get from here to there yet. It's an important step in making it real.

4. **What are the most challenging life experiences you've overcome?**
    Determine what they are and describe how they've shaped you. These stumbling blocks often become stepping stones to your future. They give you special insight and experiences that lead you to decisions about your calling.

5. **What are the things you do because you're passionate about them?**
    These are activities where your creativity blossoms and time passes quickly. You smile when you think about these topics and can excitedly talk to others about them at length. You may fall asleep at night or wake up in the morning thinking about these things. Others might think of them as work, but for you they're energizing and enjoyable.

The Next Step

It may take you weeks or even months to think though and write down your responses to these questions. Sometimes it's like peeling away the layers of an onion as you go through the process of discovery. The only wrong answer is the one that comes from thinking about what *others* expect you to say and do, and not being truthful to *yourself*. When you've reached the point of breakthrough, you'll know it because you'll have an "aha" moment. Then it's a matter of making sure decisions about your work align with your understanding of your purpose. It's a step-by-step process. Often, as you get closer, you recognize even more opportunity for greater impact. Working in your calling brings you to the top of Abraham Maslow's "hierarchy of needs," or self-actualization, where you're achieving your full potential.

Now is the time to take the journey to *finding you* and **pivot to purpose**.

3. PURPOSE, PATIENCE, AND PREPARATION
Five Principles for Success

"Patience is not passively waiting. Patience is active acceptance of the process required to achieve your goals and dreams."

—RAY DAVIS, AUTHOR

Everyone has a purpose, but not everyone will recognize and fulfill it. And one of the biggest reasons why is because they won't have the patience to go through the process and see it come to pass.

Joe is a good example of how practicing patience and preparation ultimately led to fulfilling his purpose. He grew up the youngest of four brothers on the family farm in the Midwest. His father owned herds of cattle. And while they weren't poor, they were far from rich. One day, Joe had a dream that he would be running a multimillion-dollar company and make a distinctive impact on millions of people. Different from any other dream, this one was vivid and clear. The next morning, he remembered every detail of his dream and couldn't shake the feeling that somehow it meant something. This dream seemed the farthest thing from reality because none of Joe's brothers had gone to college or left the family business, and there was no expectation that he would either.

25

When Joe was in his late teens, his father died suddenly. Joe had never had a good relationship with his older brothers, and once his father was gone, his brothers made it clear they didn't want him around. He always had different ideas on how to run the farm, ideas they didn't support. Although his father was patient and saw the value in his proposals, they didn't.

Dejected and grieving, Joe decided to move several hundred miles away to the city and find a job. He was fortunate to find a position working in a manufacturing plant. While there, his management skills and his ability to quickly learn the business and apply innovative approaches caught the eye of his boss. He was promoted a number of times over the course of the next 10 years until he became the plant manager, responsible for hundreds of millions of dollars in revenue.

Then, one day, the owner came to Joe, furious because a recent audit uncovered that someone had altered the plant financial records and siphoned off millions of dollars. Unfortunately, all evidence pointed to Joe. While it wasn't true, and he suspected his operations manager was the culprit, he had no proof. Joe was indicted, convicted, and sentenced to 20 years in prison.

In prison, the warden recognized Joe's strong management skills and entrusted him to literally run the prison operations. Even the guards came to him for direction on how to handle certain situations. One day, a prominent businessman entered the prison system, also wrongfully convicted of a crime. He and Joe became friends as they discussed various business strategies. This businessman had powerful attorneys appealing his conviction, and within six months they were successful in having it overturned and gaining his release. Joe asked the businessman to help him gain his release, too.

Years passed and the businessman forgot about Joe, but Joe continued to faithfully work for the warden, learning and ensuring that the prison was run efficiently. By this time, the businessman's company was in severe financial trouble due to an economic downturn. As he was thinking about the changes he needed to make in his leadership team to achieve a strategic shift, he remembered the bright, young man he met in prison, with his unique perspective and ideas. As far-fetched as it seemed, the businessman knew he needed Joe to join his team. But was it possible to get him out of prison?

He instructed his attorneys to dig into why Joe was there in the first place. They discovered that the original attorneys handling Joe's case had not thoroughly investigated the situation and were able to uncover evidence leading to the real perpetrator. Joe was subsequently released from prison and his conviction was overturned. He was free!

The businessman then hired Joe to be the COO of his company. Joe employed those same strategies discussed years earlier while the two were in prison and he turned the company around. Within three years, company revenues doubled. Joe became a well-respected leader in the industry, known for innovative approaches and sound management practices.

Joe had no legitimate reason to believe he would accomplish his dream. He didn't have the educational pedigree like so many others in similar positions. He didn't grow up in the right social circles. He didn't work his way up the corporate ladder. But he was able to employ the skills he learned on the farm in a different setting.

Patience and Preparation

Joe also demonstrated two important qualities that optimized growth as part of his purpose: patience and preparation. Patience is accepting delay without letting your emotions drive negative behavior. Individuals with patience try to learn while they wait. Exercising patience confirms that you move forward in your purpose at the right time, based on your ability and maturity to handle it.

Preparation is what you do while you're being patient. This is when you focus on the experiences in front of you, even when they don't quite seem relevant to your purpose. Often, you'll find the applicability of these experiences becomes clearer with time. You will also realize the road to your purpose may take far longer and be more painful and difficult than you think it should be. But it's all part of the process.

Importantly, patience and preparation teach you five key principles of purpose.

1. **Capability**

    Just because you know your purpose doesn't mean you possess the skill set to fulfill it.

2. **Timing**

    Just because you know your purpose doesn't mean the timing is right to move forward with it.

3. **Process**

    Just because you know your purpose doesn't mean that you know the right steps to take to manifest it.

4. **Perspective**

    Just because you know your purpose, doesn't mean you fully comprehend it.

5. **Impact**

    Just because you know your purpose doesn't mean you will understand the outcome of it yet.

As you consider the glimpse of your future, the inkling of your purpose, you know it likely won't be easy to get there. You probably will experience setbacks, but embracing and learning from those difficulties will make you stronger and more effective. Use these principles to understand the importance of patience and preparation so you can walk into your life's purpose.

4. DOING NOTHING
The Biggest Risk

"If you're unwilling to risk the unusual,
you'll have to settle for the ordinary."

—JIM ROHN, ENTREPRENEUR, AUTHOR,
AND MOTIVATIONAL SPEAKER

There's a well-known parable about a wealthy CEO who took an extended business trip and left his company in the hands of his three vice presidents. He gave each of them a portion of his assets to manage in his absence. Based on what he knew of their capabilities, he gave the first one, whom we'll call Pat, $50 million to manage. The next one, Chris, was given $20 million. The third one, Joe, was given $10 million.

When the CEO returned two years later, he asked for a report of the three vice presidents' activities and earnings during his absence. Pat proudly showed him how she had shrewdly doubled the assets entrusted to her and now had $100 million. Chris was similarly pleased to show that he had $40 million. By now Joe realized he had fallen far short of his CEO's expectations. Afraid to take a risk in losing his leader's money since, after all, he couldn't afford to pay it back, he did absolutely nothing with it. Nothing. Joe didn't even try to put it in a "safe," low-return investment. You can imagine how the CEO dealt with Joe after that.

Rut versus Risk

Pat and Chris could probably tell some interesting stories about their journey to doubling their assets, things they learned along the way both about *themselves* and their *business strategies*. They likely experienced some failures too, but they were able to effectively *manage* to get through them.

Joe, on the other hand, was afraid to take any type of risk with the valuable resources that had been entrusted to him. He simply sat on them. Surely he had an idea of a business strategy he could try, something he wanted to do, but unfortunately, he didn't know how to do it or was afraid to take the risk. And by doing nothing, Joe effectively lost ground.

There are too many people like Joe, stuck in the ruts of demonstrating ineffective leadership behaviors, producing negative business results, performing unfulfilling work, and facing unrealized dreams and goals. These individuals have found the so-called *comfort* of their present state to be more powerful than the *energy* required to change. They've become paralyzed at the prospect of failure or embarrassment, or having to deploy a new strategy or learn a new skill, and are not yet willing to put forth the effort to get out of their rut. Think about the process of getting a vehicle out of a rut. Living in the snow belt, I learned as a teenager how to shift a vehicle between drive and reverse and gun the motor to rock it out. (It was actually fun!) Doing nothing and staying in that rut wasn't an option.

No Risk, No Progress

Olympic athletes provide a stark example of individuals who push themselves to higher levels of achievement. If they really want to win gold, they have to exceed past accomplishments and risk personal, physical injury to see how far their minds and bodies can go. The psychological component is as great as the physical component in reaching their goal. There are definite downside risks for their commitment: training expenses, loss of family time and typical teenage activities, unflattering public relations and social media feedback, the emotional toll of their grueling schedule, and obviously, failure to qualify for the games.

But the bottom line is that a life without risk is a life without progress. Accomplishing anything of significance requires risk. And yet it's important to understand that taking a risk doesn't always mean you'll achieve a specifically articulated goal. Most of the athletes who strive for the Olympics never get there. Ninety-six percent of businesses fail within 10 years after startup.[6] Many organizational transformations and business reorganizations fail. Their fault lies not in *taking* a risk, but in *managing* that risk effectively.

Managing Risk

Managing risk requires certain competencies: flexibility, adaptability, being proactive, learning agility, and the ability to make quality decisions. It also requires a deep knowledge of your subject matter and business environment, a willingness to learn from others, and a clear understanding of the potential downsides. In the midst of all of that, you also must forgive yourself when you make a mistake, because you will.

Most leaders will have to face high-stakes risks during their careers. Here are just a few examples:

- **Making decisions that can have a negative impact on your career**
  How will your employment be negatively affected by this decision? What's your potential loss of professional reputation or your capability of finding the right, next job quickly? What's the financial impact on you and your family?

- **Answering to stakeholders**
  If your company's new product or service doesn't meet established revenue goals, how will your stakeholders (investors, clients, board, sponsors, family) respond?

■ **Starting a new business**

If you invest in this new business venture and it fails, how will you deal with it?

The bottom line is, don't pour all your resources into a high-risk strategy unless you can afford to lose everything. Be smart about the risks you take, but take more than you turn down and learn from those you take. Choose the right career path. Find a new position that aligns with your values. Master new leadership skills. Lead an innovative program for your company. Pursue your purpose. Invest in a viable business idea. Step out of your rut.

Risk is a growth word. Anything of value that is gained has come through the risk of failure. Doing nothing is not an option.

6. Bill Carmody, "Why 96 Percent of Businesses Fail Within 10 Years," *Inc.*, August 12, 2015, https://www.inc.com/bill-carmody/why-96-of-businesses-fail-within-10-years.html.

5. MAKING A SHIFT
Strategic Reinvention

"There is at least one point in the history of any company when you have to change dramatically to rise to the next level of performance. Miss that moment and you start to decline."

—ANDY GROVE, FORMER CEO OF INTEL

Steve Ballmer had a new lease on life. After more than three decades at Microsoft as employee number 30, he retired as CEO in February 2014 and was looking toward the future. He was also ranked highly on *Forbes'* list of wealthiest Americans. So he discussed his plans for the future with writer George Anders.[7]

Ballmer expected his recent purchase of the Los Angeles Clippers to take a large chunk of his time. It was his third attempt to purchase an NBA team and many believed he overpaid for the opportunity. But the new venture aligned with his love of the sport and focused him in an entirely different direction. Although Ballmer is no longer involved with Microsoft, as the company's largest individual shareholder (over 300 million shares as of the date of this interview!) he will continue to closely monitor his investment. He has also used his vast experience to teach MBA students at the Stanford

33

Graduate School of Business, discussing the successes and failures of his former company.

Finally, and more importantly, Ballmer and his wife decided to make plans to use their formidable wealth to positively impact society through philanthropy. He surrounded himself with a group of advisors to understand issues and problems around the world as he formulated his next steps in this arena. Ballmer's legendary energy level—evidenced whenever he met with employees at Microsoft and with Clippers fans at his first game as owner—seemed at an all-time high as he looked toward the future. He made a shift to strategically reinvent himself.

Organizational Reinvention

Ballmer's exit from Microsoft came during a period when investors were calling for change. Given the pressures on new product development and revenue, it was time for a shift in the company. He had reached a senior level of professional maturity and accomplishment, and it was time to look for the next shift in his own life. Granted, 99.99 percent of the population aren't quite as rich or accomplished as Ballmer, but nonetheless, they are similarly passionate about their past and future, and they reach a point in life where they need a shift...a strategic reinvention.

IBM faced such a pivotal moment several years ago. In their 2014 third quarter earnings release, CEO Virginia Rometty acknowledged a need to reinvent the company just 20 years after its strategic shift from hardware to software and computer services.[8] Revenues had declined for the tenth straight quarter, business lines were lagging, and the company was warning that it would miss an earnings target. Some described IBM as an "old technology company" that needed to quickly move into cloud computing. Although opinions varied, IBM was obviously in need of a shift...a strategic reinvention.

How to Get There

Making a shift, or a strategic reinvention, is characterized by several phases. It typically starts when continuing the same behavior or activities is no longer an option and there's a broader recognition of the need for new and different approaches. Often the way forward isn't clear, but as the leader moves through each of the following stages, the next steps become evident.

■ **Discomfort**

When individual or organizational results are no longer as favorable, and the tried and true strategies to improve them don't work, this is a warning signal. There may be an uneasiness that the environment is changing, stakeholders want different outcomes, and competitive requirements are fluctuating. The ability to develop plans to meet future needs becomes more difficult as the environment lacks clarity.

■ **Direction**

Strategic reinvention requires thoughtful evaluation of where you want to go, what you want to become, and whether you have the resources to get there. It takes careful assessment of the competitive environment, the financial requirements, the skill set of your team, the time necessary for change, and future perspective. Reinvention entails a level of resolve by the leader to make tough decisions unencumbered by the past and being able to head in the right direction.

■ **Destination**

Where you end up after a strategic reinvention will obviously look different from where you were. The people who were with you in the past may not follow you into the future because they are not capable of making the shift; they're not invested in the change.

Your destination can represent a fresh start, a new beginning, a different approach to how you add value to others. It's important to take advantage of the momentum you gather along the way and carefully construct the environment crucial to your success.

- **Duration**

  Change takes time because it's largely the process of individuals or groups of people seeing themselves differently. We become invested in the current image we have of ourselves or our organizations, even when it no longer produces the best results. Thus, the change is really about developing a new image, learning new skills that are within our capability, and thinking differently about our roles and responsibilities. Shifting into a new vision of ourselves and our organizations can be emotionally or psychologically painful, so it may take time.

The Winds of Change

Former Intel CEO Andy Grove's book, *Only the Paranoid Survive*, makes the point that we all need to be open to the winds of change. These winds will require us to shift gears and experience a strategic reinvention so that we can move further faster. And it's rarely easy. Often a coach, advisor, or consultant with specific expertise in your area of focus can help guide you on the pathway as you find your pace in shifting gears. Ultimately, all of us will need to shift. How will you handle it?

7. George Anders, "Gone from Microsoft, Ballmer Begins a Surprising Second Act," *Forbes*, September 30, 2014, http://www.forbes.com/sites/georgeanders/2014/09/30/steve-ballmers-zesty-new-life-23-5-billion-and-an-nba-team/.

8. Don Clark, "IBM Woes Point to a Fresh Overhaul," *The Wall Street Journal*, October 20, 2014, http://online.wsj.com/articles/ibm-to-transfer-chip-ops-as-revenue-drops-again-1413804259.

LEADERSHIP PURPOSE REFLECTIONS

By now you realize that understanding your leadership purpose requires considerable reflection and investment of time. It also requires discipline to avoid what's called the "shiny pebbles on the side of the road"—distractions with no lasting value—and instead focus on the long road ahead. Understanding and pursuing your leadership purpose will be challenging, but in the long run will provide you with greater personal satisfaction and contribute more effectively to team and organizational outcomes.

Here are the reflection questions on **Leadership Purpose**:

◆ What is your purpose for leading?

◆ You may be enjoying your career, but is this your calling?

◆ How is your current role preparing you to move toward your purpose in life? And how do you need to demonstrate patience to get there?

◆ Where do you need to get out of a rut, take a risk, and make progress in working toward your purpose?

◆ What winds of change are blowing in your life?

The answers may not all come right away, but they will come eventually.

Step 2.

Foundational viewpoints to guide leaders

Leadership **Perspective** is the foundational viewpoint that helps to guide leaders' decisions. It drives how they think about and approach work and relate to colleagues. This vantage point challenges them to rethink previous assumptions and thought processes, to practice curiosity, and to broaden their outlook on their approach to leadership.

If you've ever gone hiking or driving through the mountains, you've seen different views of the same terrain and observed the same objects from different perspectives. When you saw the same thing from different angles and distances, you learned more about it. In your work, you're probably used to seeing business issues and opportunities from the same perspective, based on data, feedback, and the routine of your monthly operating reviews and processes. But what if you gained a different perspective on these issues? Try asking your stakeholders; bring in different experts; ask amateurs; find people who have different personality styles or preferences; go to a different geographic region; brainstorm 50 questions; or think of six different ways to address the problem. Do anything other than what you normally do, so you can be open to new possibilities. A new perspective can open up new business approaches and solutions to perplexing problems.

1. DEVELOPING LEADERSHIP PERSPECTIVE
Fact versus Reality

"Those who look only to the past or the present are certain to miss the future."

—JOHN F. KENNEDY, 35TH PRESIDENT
OF THE UNITED STATES

There's an old fable about three blind men who touched an elephant to find out what it was like. One man touched the leg and declared the elephant was like a tree trunk. Another touched the elephant's tail and declared it was like a snake. The third man touched its side and declared it was like a wall. A disagreement ensued as they each defended their perspective on the animal. After all, they knew what they felt.

Were each of them right? Yes, and no. They each experienced a part of the elephant, but none experienced the whole. They each described the elephant from their perspective, but due to limitations in their vision and space, none of them could visualize it in its entirety. Later, a sighted man came along and immediately saw the whole elephant. He quickly walked around the animal, sized it up, and fully described it to the men, connecting their diverse experiences. While they were each correct, their *facts* didn't describe the complete picture. They didn't describe *reality*.

Fact versus Reality

A similar situation occurs in many aspects of leadership as well. Here are a few examples.

During organizational problem solving, people can "describe the facts" based on their perspective of a situation, each being "correct" in some way. But the reality of that situation is far more multifaceted. Leaders seeking to understand the issue must research and investigate it from all angles to get a proper perspective of the circumstances and develop the right strategy for the company.

Leaders from different departments of an organization see business problems like sagging sales, dissatisfied customers, poor product quality, or employee disengagement from different perspectives. Based on their respective areas of expertise, the culture and politics, and their personal styles, they *individually* point to different factors contributing to the problem. But only when they *collectively* analyze the situation can they recognize the complexity and interdependent parts that must be understood to arrive at the most appropriate solution.

Consider that when faced with unpopular business decisions, such as layoffs or elimination of products and services, stakeholders (i.e., employees, clients, suppliers, investors, and the community) often respond based on their personal impact. They typically have a limited set of facts and lack the broader perspective of the leader in understanding the reasons driving the change. In these situations, leaders have a responsibility to evaluate and communicate decisions in the context of those impacted by the changes. For example, the workforce in a manufacturing facility should receive regular state-of-the-business updates about consumer demand for their products, quality issues, competitive threats, cost drivers, and other key business factors. If the plant leadership subsequently reduces the number of employees, these are indicators the leaders must use to explain that decision. Leaders must also clarify how those decisions link to the organization's overall values and objectives.

Developing Perspective

As leaders, we are naturally a bit like the blind men. We initially experience an organization, an issue, a person, or an event from a limited viewpoint. We don't have all the information and must be careful to avoid quick decisions or snap judgements based on partial knowledge. We don't know the history or how the past fits into the future and must avoid making long-term pronouncements with short-term evidence. We need perspective, and the first step in developing it is *awareness* of our restricted vision. The next step is *action*, to gain an understanding of the full environment impacting our work. Here are actions you can take:

1. **Be well read** on trends, competitive threats, and new ideas in your space. Maintain a healthy curiosity about what's happening around you and be open to innovative approaches.

2. **Invite input** from a broad cross section of stakeholders. This group should include people internal and external to your organization, whose knowledge and expertise can help you see the entire picture.

3. **Think systemically** about interrelationships and patterns. Be able to connect the dots and understand the impact one situation has on other areas. The butterfly effect theory posits that a small change in one area of a system can cause a huge impact elsewhere in the system.

4. **Develop high emotional intelligence** to understand the nuances in your environment. High emotional intelligence includes showing empathy, managing your emotions, demonstrating social skills, and understanding the culture of the organization around you.

5. **Wear trifocals** to take in multiple viewpoints. Look at situations from 100,000 feet (strategic view), 50,000 feet (process view), and sometimes 10,000 feet (tactical view) to ensure you have a clear picture of what is occurring and the impact of your decisions.

As we develop perspective, we gain vision that extends beyond the normal range and expands broader than our current role and situation. Proper leadership perspective takes the long-term view, where *present* situations are understood in the context of the *past* and as a setup for the *future*.

So where can you benefit from developing a broader leadership perspective?

2. MANAGING RISK
Priorities and Decisions

*"Business people need to understand the psychology
of risk more than the mathematics of risk."*

—PAUL GIBBONS, AUTHOR, SPEAKER, AND CONSULTANT
ON POST-TRUTH, SCIENCE AND SOCIETY, SCIENCE
AND CHANGE, BUSINESS ETHICS, AND PHILOSOPHY

B ob sat down at his desk and let out a huge sigh. He had just
returned from lunch with one of the board members at his company. They were preparing for the current CEO to retire within the
next six months and the board wanted to initiate a formal selection
process to confirm Bob as a candidate to replace him. Bob had been
with the company for 15 years and held the CFO role for five years. It
was time to step up. He knew the inner workings of the company, as
well as challenges in the industry. He also knew that his chances of
being selected were pretty good.

But there was one nagging issue on Bob's mind. He fundamentally felt that the strategy the current CEO and board were pursuing
wasn't going to pay off the way they thought. He had shared his concerns in the past, but given the politics, he didn't feel he could push it
too far. If he were to be selected CEO, he realized he couldn't lead the
organization forward with a strategy he didn't believe in. He knew two
or three of the 11 board members might support his thinking, but that

wasn't sufficient to make the shift he felt was necessary. And if he declined consideration, he'd have to come up with a really good reason, because telling them he didn't believe in their strategy would call into question his role over the past several years.

If someone else were chosen as CEO, Bob wasn't sure their interpersonal dynamics or opinion on running the business would be aligned. Plus, if the new leader determined a different strategy was in order, he might bring in his own CFO anyway, thinking Bob either wasn't the right fit or that the first runner-up for the CEO position wouldn't be loyal to the selected one. Bob either needed to step up and go for it or leave.

Bob was in just one of many situations over the course of his 30-year career where he needed to navigate organizational and environmental politics. He had a few scars from the past, but he prided himself on his ability to bounce back, build and maintain strong relationships with the board members, and avoid some of the missteps of his peers. This might be the pivotal point, however. And as only his wife knew, Bob wasn't even sure he really wanted to be CEO! He knew his own strengths, passions, and weaker areas, and though the title sounded great, he really preferred and operated best in the CFO role. So he was now at the pinnacle of the riskiest point in his career.

But Bob's risk didn't begin when he was asked to consider the CEO role, it began years earlier. That's when he contributed to defining the company strategy and didn't voice his concerns in a persuasive enough manner to ensure they were heard and not minimized.

The Risks We Confront

Successful careers come with an ongoing series of professional and personal risks to be managed. The ability to chart a course through land mines, quicksand, and potholes requires skill and insight sprinkled with a lot of chance, none of which ever aligns perfectly. And the reality is, a poor decision in one area may easily impact another.

These decisions related to managing a myriad of risks impact us on a daily basis. The following are typical examples of these situations:

■ **What job do I accept?**
You research, network, and gain as much information as possible about the position, leadership, culture, compensation, responsibilities, and career growth prospects, then take a risk on your decision.

■ **Who do I align myself with politically in the organization?**
When leaders adopt conflicting positions, or have negative interpersonal dynamics, their team members or others in the organization may feel forced to take sides. Sometimes staying in "Switzerland" or being neutral isn't possible, especially the farther you move up the ranks.

■ **What is my personal brand?**
Decisions about your area of specialization or expertise, visual presence, networks, professional approach, and how you leverage your strengths will expose you to some opportunities and eliminate others.

■ **What's my summary recommendation on a project?**
In the midst of political positioning on controversial issues, you may feel pressure to present a recommendation that minimizes safety issues, maximizes profits, or downplays quality issues.

■ **Should I support my work friend even though my other peers don't believe she's adding much value to the organization?**
When work politics don't align with your personal choice of friends, you may be forced to choose whether to support your friend's candidacy for a position or agree with another point of view.

- **How do I show up at my new job?**
  The way you transition into the workplace, set priorities with your new team, or work with a coach to become acclimated can make all the difference in a successful start.

    Your approach to managing each of these scenarios is driven by your priorities, values, and decision quality.

How We Manage Risk

Recognizing that these risks are inherent by virtue of being in an organization, you have to try to manage your options and minimize problematic issues. There are a few ground rules to guide your behavior.

- **Identify priorities and values.**
  Know what you stand for. Clarify your values. They will be challenged regularly, and if you don't first know what you stand for, you won't be able to respond appropriately.

- **Properly recognize where risk exists.**
  This is part of being politically savvy and sensitive to how individuals and organizations operate. You have to anticipate issues, be able to differentiate the potholes (smaller consequences) from the land mines (major consequences), and navigate effectively.

- **Anticipate probabilities.**
  Part of this planning includes determining the likelihood of a negative or positive consequence occurring.

- **Determine mitigating responses.**
  Being proactive to address the risk includes building coalitions and support, getting advice from a mentor or sponsor, and effectively weighing the pros and cons.

Most importantly, understand that you can't anticipate all of your future risks. So you must navigate carefully. Build professional relationships on the basis of integrity. Avoid saying things about colleagues behind their backs that you wouldn't share with them face-to-face. Share and document your professional recommendations and insights with respect for others' opinions. Bravely stand up for issues of safety, quality, and fairness. And at the end of the day, be prepared to live with your decisions, even if they aren't popular.

Managing risk is not to be confused with avoiding it. You are guaranteed to find yourself in risky situations. But managing risk means measuring and accepting it, and being willing to face it head on, responsibly.

3. IMPORTANT VERSUS URGENT
10 Important Questions for Leaders

*"The art and science of asking questions
is the source of all knowledge."*

—THOMAS BERGER, BEST-SELLING AUTHOR

J eff was exhausted. Six months after assuming the role as CEO of a midsize manufacturing company, he felt like he was treading water yet slowly drowning. As CFO for the past 10 years, he was very familiar with the company's operational and financial challenges and presented a convincing growth strategy during his interview with the board selection committee. The position he sought was finally his, but now, sitting in the corner office was a bit different than he anticipated. Competing internal demands and external market volatility increased the daily complexities of managing the business. Every day there was a new emergency. Jeff now recognized how optimistic yet naïve he was in believing he could more quickly implement his plans. He realized that he needed to think more deeply about the underlying factors impacting the organization, and engage his leadership team in reviewing their priorities.

Jeff's situation was not unusual. One of his most important learnings was that he needed to step back from the myriad of *urgent* issues and focus on those that are *important*. He needed to achieve a balance between being in a *reactionary* crisis mode and a *proactive* planning mode, understand the underlying causes, and implement the right plans for the organization. He also had to pause and reflect on how he, as the leader, was influencing behaviors to ensure the right outcomes. This would require him to fundamentally shift the way he led the team, but he knew in his heart it was a strategic change that would determine his leadership success.

Leaders who shift their attention to the *important* issues in their companies benefit by engaging with their teams on 10 crucial questions. The answers to these questions will form the basis of their strategies for growth.

1. **Purpose: WHY *are you doing what you're doing?***

   Many organizations and teams shift into automatic mode as their activities become routinized. They assume demand will continue for their products and services, and they evolve into placing more focus on *what* they're doing or *how* they're doing it, instead of WHY they're doing it. But asking the question WHY connects you to the purpose of your activities. WHY is the motivator and driving force that inspires your team to take appropriate action that will support your goal. Once they understand your WHY, an emotional link can form as your team members pinpoint their contribution to accomplishing what you desire to achieve.

   The underlying WHY of an individual, team, or organization typically does not change because it becomes a core belief. According to Simon Sinek, the *how* and *what* changes as necessary to continue to support the WHY. When you know your purpose— or your WHY—and communicate it effectively, this clarity attracts others to you who also want to support that objective.

2. **Disruption: *What is the disruptive threat to your business model?***

   Leaders should be constantly aware of ongoing threats to their business model and its products or services and take action to address them. Make a list of all the products and services provided by your organization, your team, and even you, based on skill sets. Now, for each one, think about two or three ways that your product, service, or skill set can be provided faster, cheaper, or differently. What technological advances might make your current products or services obsolete? How might consumer preferences shift away from your current model? Believe in the possibility and probability of this disruption, then focus on the future and how you'll address that threat. Shift your business model to where your customers are going instead of where they are now. Jim Kennedy, chairman of Cox Enterprises, provided a great example of this when he diversified his family business away from classified ads to leverage the growing role of the Internet by successfully launching Autotrader.com in 1997.

3. **Failure: *Where have you failed and what insights have you learned from that failure?***
   If you've never failed, you've never attempted something of impact and significance relative to your abilities. Failure can add value when you learn something from it and build upon it. Thomas Edison failed many times in trying to develop a light bulb. The Wright brothers failed before leveraging their underdog status to become the first in flight. J.C. Penney was sick and bankrupt before he built his namesake store into a retailing giant. But they all learned from their failures, kept trying, and eventually succeeded.

   Failure is only bad if you fall into shame and shut down afterwards. Instead, find a stepping stone to move forward. Failure is generally a precursor to growth—finding what *doesn't* work until you find what *does* work. It's accompanied by exploration, curiosity, pursuit, action, and flexibility. And most importantly, it should involve reflecting on and learning lessons that can be applied to other situations and constructively shared with others.

4. **Curiosity: *What are you curious about?***
   Curiosity is a precursor to learning. Though it's easy to be consumed with the daily challenges of leadership roles, it's important to take

time to explore insights in related areas to stimulate your thought processes and spur new ideas. Research shows that successful CEOs are curious, and this curiosity leads to growth.

Mark Zuckerberg, CEO of Facebook, started his Year of Books online reading club in 2015 to encourage discovery about different beliefs, cultures, and technologies. And Richard Kinder, Chairman and CEO of Kinder Morgan reads about 50 books a year. He learns how other leaders have confronted challenges, particularly overwhelming ones for which they had few ready answers. His curiosity in reading is linked to his interests and fuels his passion for learning. So, dig into those areas that you're curious about and your learning will form the basis for future growth. Even if your reading interests are unrelated to your work, they may provide a needed break to help clear your mind and create opportunities for new ideas.

5. **Service: What does my team need from me in order for them to be successful?**

As a leader, your responsibility is to serve your employees, enabling them, in turn, to provide value to customers, investors, and the community. You serve your team by creating a compelling vision and providing the processes, tools, and structure to support innovation, recognition, teamwork, and success. Service requires a continual focus on others to understand their needs, motivations, and aspirations, and to provide them with opportunities for growth. This includes a measure of humility to steer the focus from your own accomplishments to the team's accomplishments, and to ensure that your decisions serve them and not yourself.

Service also provides a greater connection to the team as you partner together in the organization's success. Leaders who focus on service take responsibility when things go wrong. Leaders who focus on service empower their teams. Leaders who focus on service attract, retain, and develop talented people.

6. **Engagement:** *How do you engage your team in what you're trying to accomplish?*

Engagement is based on an emotional connection that energizes those involved to work toward a common goal. Competitive rowing teams, known as "scullers" or "sweep rowers," require all rowers to move in exact cadence with the leader for an efficient stroke. The leader is responsible for steering the boat, encouraging the crew, and monitoring the rate of progress. Everyone knows their role and whom to follow, and this engagement is an important key to winning. Contrast that unified effort with a scenario where everyone is rowing at their own pace. They're working at it, and they'll make progress, but not nearly as fast because their behaviors aren't aligned within the team.

Similarly, as the leader, you must ensure your team clearly understands the goal and that their efforts are coordinated, collaborative, and complementary. This means making sure they buy into why the goal is important and they contribute their ideas on how to best accomplish it. Team members who have the opportunity to offer suggestions will feel more engaged and committed to the end result.

7. **Innovation:** *Are you creating an environment that encourages new thinking?*

Innovation involves taking existing ideas, processes, or products and combining them in new and different ways to meet customer or market needs. For example, electric vehicles are innovative. Some companies have innovation labs or innovation hours (i.e., hackathons), but this approach ultimately needs to be embedded in the culture of the organization. New ideas must be nurtured and encouraged.

Carl Winans, cofounder of Mega Tiny Corporation, asks an interesting question: "Are you creating or merely consuming?" In other words, do you integrate information and knowledge to provide new and different output that is beneficial to others? Or do you just take it and use it? Leaders' interactions with employees should incorporate discussions on innovative topics, solicit ideas, encourage them to investigate the potential for success, and when appropriate, give them a leadership role in operationalizing their ideas. This rewards innovation and reinforces the skills requisite for success.

8. **Power: *Do people follow you because of your power and position or because you empower them?***
   If you were no longer CEO, vp, or holding your current leadership position, who among your team would still want to follow you? John Maxwell's book, *The 5 Levels of Leadership*, explains that at level 1, people follow you because they have to. But as you move to level 5, people follow you because of who you are and what you represent. You only have power with others to the extent that they grant it to you, whether through an employment relationship or because you meet a financial, emotional, social, psychological, or physical need. Once you cease to fulfill that need, or they find someone else to fulfill it, you become effectively powerless. On the other hand, as a leader you can *empower* others, or give power to *them* by providing them with responsibility, enabling them to do something, or equipping them to accomplish a challenge. Giving power to others generates a virtuous cycle of enabling, growth, commitment and engagement.

9. **Performance: *What is the correlation between your effort and your outcomes?***
   This is a sensitive issue, because all leaders like to believe that they're exceeding the expectations of the individuals or groups to whom they're accountable (and we're all accountable to someone). But there are enough situations where no matter how intellectually capable or strategic the leader, their best efforts don't move the needle forward as much as is needed or expected. Is their skill set incomplete? Is the internal business challenge too great? Are there insurmountable, external economic or market forces that can't be overcome?

Marissa Mayer joined Yahoo in 2012 as its fifth CEO since 2007 amid great fanfare about how she could turn the struggling company around. While she was credited with improving product design and driving increased traffic, several costly acquisitions didn't yield meaningful financial returns.[9] Three years later, the company had to scrap its plans to spin off its extremely valuable stake in Alibaba Group Holding and investors began to demand changes in the company's management and strategy. Two massive security breaches added to the company's quandary and Yahoo was eventually purchased by Verizon.

It's unclear how much of the outcome was due to Mayer's capability versus the state of the business and environment. But the performance question is one that every leader grapples with at some point. And if the effort is not producing the right outcomes, it may be time for the leader to find a new opportunity where their contributions will align with strong results.

10. **Change:** *Are you leading your organization to be nimble, flexible, and open to change?*

Change doesn't happen unless the leader makes it a priority. When Nikesh Arora (who as of this writing is the CEO and Chairman of Palo Alto Networks) was hired in 2004 to run Google's European operations, he doubled his initial five-year revenue projection for the region and created the analytical tools that were eventually implemented to track the financial condition of the global business. He was tough, but his enemies respected him. Instead of changing his leadership style to fit into the company, Arora shrewdly changed the organization's leadership perspective to mirror his own. During his tenure at Google, Arora rose to become senior vice president and chief business officer, responsible for almost $30 billion in revenue. His philosophy was "anytime you can predict your trajectory, you should change it."[10]

Leaders who direct change don't wait for external forces to direct internal business strategies. They anticipate the market, technologies, economy, and customer needs. They develop a flexible framework and goals for the future. Then they ensure the right processes, strategies, technologies, and tools are in place to get there.

By now you recognize that these questions and their associated capabilities are interdependent with one another to achieve individual and organizational success. Your challenge is to identify those that are most important to *your* growth and develop learning strategies to improve in those areas.

9. Miguel Helft, "The Last Days of 'Marissa Mayer?," *Forbes*, November 19, 2015, http://www.forbes.com/sites/miguelhelft/2015/11/19/the-last-days-of-marissa-mayer/.

10. Erin Griffith, "Can Nikesh Aurora Make Softbank the Berkshire Hathaway of Tech?," *Fortune*, December 3, 2015, http://fortune.com/nikesh-arora-softbank-startups/.

4. GAINING A NEW PERSPECTIVE
5 Steps to Reset Your View

*"If you change the way you look at things,
the things you look at change."*

—DR. WAYNE DYER, INTERNATIONALLY RENOWNED
AUTHOR AND SPEAKER IN THE FIELDS OF
SELF-DEVELOPMENT AND SPIRITUAL GROWTH

Think about a time when you were in the midst of an important challenge, working on a major project, or slogging through solving a pervasive problem. Then you hit a wall. Your burst of energy and creativity dissipated. Your initial, accelerated progress slowed to a snail's pace. You and your team were stuck and found it difficult to break through to the next level of innovation and advancement. How did you move forward? You needed a new perspective. You needed to look at the challenge from a different angle, using a different lens, with a fresh set of eyes.

Unfortunately, too often we waste time pressing forward working on a solution just to show activity, while in reality we're making minimal headway. A more effective use of our time is to proactively take specific steps to gain a different perspective. When we anticipate the diminishing return on our effort, we can pause and make a shift in our approach to ensure maximum productivity.

What Do You Do Next?

1. **Take a break.**

   Stop what you're doing. Put it down. Walk away—for five minutes, an hour, a day, or a week—for as long as practical. At some point you've become so immersed in your project that your initial burst of inspiration has faded and you need to give your mind a break. Focus on other things. Gain inspiration from some seemingly unrelated activities and topics. Don't underestimate the value of a vacation, staycation, doing something fun, or just utilizing the opposite side of your brain. You may find new ideas will come to you when you're in the midst of a totally unrelated activity, or when you return to the task at hand you'll simply be refreshed from spending time away from it.

   And make sure you're getting enough sleep. A study of 27 CEOs' daily schedules by Harvard Business School professors Michael Porter and Nitin Nohria revealed that on average, in a 24-hour period, those CEOs spent seven hours sleeping and 10 hours working.[11] According to another *Harvard Business Review* study, the higher the level of senior executives, the more sleep they get.[12] So don't think that your ability to work nonstop for extended hours is a positive trait.

2. **Invite input from others.**

   While you always want the smartest minds working on a project, those same smart minds can also be a hindrance when they approach problem-solving in a consistent way every time. Instead, think of the people who are stakeholders for the solution and then determine how to involve them. Some companies send researchers into the homes and environments of consumers to observe how they interact with their product. One example is the laundry soap container that now sits tipped on its side in my cabinet over the washing machine. I just push the button to dispense soap into a cup, instead of having to lift the entire jug and tip it over.

Even better, invite someone who has no understanding of your product or service and let them interact with it or ask questions about it. They will challenge your assumptions. Toymakers do this by giving kids prototypes to play with to see how they interact with the toy. Maybe you think this is fine for someone else's project, but yours is so special, technical, or complex that requesting input from those with no knowledge about it won't work. You may want to reconsider that idea.

3. **Sit in a different chair.**

Literally. How many times do you go to the same meeting in the same room and sit in just about the same chair? We're creatures of habit because it minimizes the number of added decisions we have to make. Instead, try sitting on the opposite side of the room, rearrange the chairs and tables, go to a different location—find a different angle from which to physically view the situation. To spur creativity, I try to hold meetings in rooms with a broad, outside view. It supports thinking expansively and imaginatively.

Professors Porter and Nohria's CEOs report spending almost half of their working time outside the office. They sit in different locations to conduct meetings with key constituencies to influence business outcomes and gain insights to drive business decisions.

4. **Assume a different point of view.**

You know the personas and points of view of individuals in your organization. What if you purposely take on one different from your own, or your team swaps personas with one another? Force yourself to think from someone else's perspective and take a position you don't normally take. Push yourself to understand the challenge differently. This means you'll have to initially get beyond all your automatic excuses as to why a point of view other than your own won't work.

Purposely forcing yourself to analyze a topic and come up with solutions to support a position you previously opposed can help you better consider new possibilities. For example, you might advocate for a different marketing strategy and in the process gain a new perspective on its benefits and potential application for your business.

5. **Spend time reflecting.**
Professors Porter and Nohria also emphasize the importance of CEOs spending time alone, thinking and being reflective about the issues they face. Stepping away from the midst of crises and everyday issues to think strategically about how to move forward can provide a fresh start, with ideas on new approaches. As I write this, I'm literally in flight, beginning a vacation and excited about the opportunity to take a pause from my normal routine to rethink and reconsider new approaches to my work. How can I work with a client differently to address a particular problem? Does a colleague's proposal to collaborate on a project fit with my business strategy? What new knowledge do I need to gain to better support my clients?

Shifting Perspective as a Practice

I practice these strategies regularly when writing and working on projects with my clients. I've learned to always allow time to take a break in the middle of an assignment and come back to it 24-72 hours later. Then I'll have new ideas and can better critique my past work. Sometimes I find a new location to work from that gives me inspiration. Since my role as a consultant affords me flexibility, I can work from a coffee shop, a coworking space, or the airport. The result is always a higher-quality outcome.

Too much of the same perspective will ultimately impede growth. Effective leaders understand the value of gaining a 360-degree view on business challenges to ensure the best results. They're not afraid to be uncomfortable, to change their approach, and to solicit participation from nontraditional sources to ensure they're driving the best solutions for the business.

What do you need to do to gain a new perspective?

11. Michael Porter and Nitin Nohria, "What Do CEOs Actually Do?," *Harvard Business Review*, July-August 2018, https://hbr.org/2018/07/the-leaders-calendar#what-do-ceos-actually-do.

12. Rasmus Hougaard and Jacqueline Carter, "Senior Executives Get More Sleep Than Everyone Else," *Harvard Business Review*, February 28, 2018, https://hbr.org/2018/02/senior-executives-get-more-sleep-than-everyone-else.

5. LEFT HAND–RIGHT HAND
Balanced Leadership

"Reason is our soul's left hand, faith her right."

—JOHN DONNE, ENGLISH POET AND CLERIC
IN THE CHURCH OF ENGLAND

Miles O'Brien[13] woke up and sensed that his left arm was there. But when he looked down, it was gone...amputated during surgery as a result of a freak injury several days prior. He wondered how he would provide for his family and perform little but important daily functions that we all take for granted. As an award-winning science journalist and CNN contributor, he traveled extensively and was an active sports enthusiast. So, what would his life be like now?

Rather than retreat into the shadows, O'Brien dove into the rehabilitation process and challenged his occupational therapists and prosthetist to support him in finding ways to continue his normal activity level. They quickly responded and helped him to fulfill his plans of traveling to the Arctic, including camping for four days on the Denali ice sheet, and riding his bicycle 300 miles across Michigan in two days. But to do so, they had to outfit him with the proper equipment and prosthesis to replace his arm. He couldn't function without a workaround strategy to replace that arm, because his body, and our bodies, must have two arms for balance.

The Power of Two

Most aspects of our daily functionality are based on having two arms. Two arms support our mobility, flexibility, and dexterity. They increase our capability to lift and carry objects, multitask, and find our equilibrium. The majority of the population is right-handed, but some (like me) are left-handed, simply indicating our ability and preference to perform more tasks with that hand. Yet even when using our preferred hand or arm, we need the other one to complement our actions. Our arms and hands are crosswired to our brains. Thus, the left side or hemisphere of our brain controls movement on the right side of our body and the right hemisphere of our brain controls movement on the left side.

Each side of our brain also has a functional specialization. For example, the left hemisphere controls mathematical, analytical, and logical processing, whereas the right hemisphere controls sensory perception, emotional processing, and artistic functions. All these processes are complementary to the full and steady functionality of our bodies and behaviors. This equilibrium is not only important for the mobility of our bodies, but the mobility of our leadership. A leader is most effective when there is a balance of skill sets and input on his or her team. A leader needs a left-hand and a right-hand mix.

The Right Hand

William Heyman[14], former vice chairman and chief investment officer of Travelers, is one of those right-hand (left hemisphere) people. During his tenure in that role, the company's stock had a 267 percent return, compared with the 109 percent return on the S&P 500. Heyman reportedly stuck to a conservative investment strategy even when the market seemed to be exploding or imploding and resisted the temptation to invest in the latest hot tip. A trusted advisor to Jay Fishman, chairman and CEO of the company, Heyman was known for his ability to think through risk and reward probabilities. He grew up around well-known investors and gained decades of Wall Street experience that positioned him for this role. Heyman provided strong analytical and logical balance to the leadership team.

The Left Hand

On the left hand (right hemisphere), Jay Fishman[15,16] had an instinct for the insurance business. He believed the most successful CEOs could sense what was going on in their business even before it showed up in the numbers. Fishman made it a point to spend time with his 13,000 independent brokers and agents, answering their questions and understanding their issues. He even attended their funerals and those of their close family members. And he encouraged his brokers and agents to spend time with their clients to ensure that they understood consumer needs.

Fishman's detailed communications with Wall Street analysts earned him plaudits for honesty and insight into the business. He built an organization that complemented his insurance instincts, allowing his team to evaluate decisions to make certain they were aligned with the company's goal. This strategy paid off, as Travelers weathered the 2008 downturn, along with massive hurricanes, tornados, and floods to deliver a decade of strong returns. Fishman's team enhanced his skill sets and provided the necessary balance for their collective leadership decisions. (Note: Fishman stepped down in 2015 due to an ALS diagnosis and passed away in 2016.)

Achieving Perfect Balance

Every leader needs individuals on his or her team to provide the predominately left-hand and right-hand perspectives in a manner that balances their thought process and decisions. Just as the brain integrates the inputs from centers of expertise in the right and left hemispheres, so must the leader seamlessly integrate these inputs from his or her team to balance and lead thoughtfully. It's a collective effort requiring coordination and agility, yet when beautifully executed demonstrates the necessary well-rounded capability to accomplish greater exploits.

13. Miles O'Brien, "My Life, Lost and Found," CNN, March 9, 2015, http://www.cnn.com/2015/03/09/opinions/obrien-life-lost-and-found/index.html.

14. Nathan Vardi, "Munificent Returns," *Forbes*, February 11, 2015, http://www.forbes.com/sites/nathanvardi/2015/02/11/munificent-returns/.

15. Nathan Vardi, "Wall Street's Honest Man," *Forbes*, February 9, 2011, https://www.forbes.com/forbes/2011/0228/features-jay-fishman-muni-bond-wall-street-honest-man.html#27724cbe1b9e.

16. Ed Leefeldt, "What If I'm Wrong?" *Leader's Edge*, October 11, 2012, http://leadersedgemagazine.com/articles/%202012/10/what-if-im-wrong.

6. INSANITY CHECK
Making Tough Decisions

"The key is not to prioritize what's on your schedule, but to schedule your priorities."

—STEPHEN COVEY, AUTHOR, *THE 7 HABITS OF HIGHLY EFFECTIVE PEOPLE*

The definition of insanity is doing the same thing over and over and expecting different results. This oft quoted statement has been attributed to a variety of people, including Albert Einstein, but it provides good motivation to evaluate our behaviors against our goals.

Many people think about making New Year's resolutions. What do they want to accomplish? What do they want to do differently? Even for those who swear off such annual declarations (many of which are only kept for a month or two), most will still take the time to pause and consider what they want to experience in the New Year. Whether or not you advocate setting resolutions, it is important to periodically assess your activities to make sure they're properly focused to support accomplishing your objectives.

This is when you take time for an *insanity check*. Evaluate your personal, professional, and organizational strategies and make the necessary adjustments to ensure you're not only making progress but attaining your goals. In what areas are you sticking to the same plan and expecting different results? What isn't working...yet? Where are you or your organization struggling? Where are you and others frustrated?

Make Tough Decisions Now

Deeply embedded problems require tough decisions. You must be willing to let go of people, processes, or products you previously invested in that are not providing sufficient return. Further delaying these decisions means you're expending and wasting valuable time in areas that won't pay off. You likely know what you must do, but you're avoiding the unpleasantness of doing it. Instead of focusing on the negative, focus on the positive outcomes.

Move your people to positions where they can add more value, or provide a bridge for them to transition outside the organization where they can find a better suited opportunity. If they're not delivering, they typically know it and are feeling some level of related stress. Avoiding the obvious issue only makes the pain worse over time.

Your team or customers will tell you which processes aren't working, if you don't already know. Set an aggressive and almost impossibly quick timetable for those processes to be fixed or eliminated. Others will thank you for it and be relieved you are finally addressing the problem.

Unprofitable *products* or *services* draw resources from the rest of the organization and literally pull others down with it. Think of a rose bush. Through careful pruning of dead or unfruitful branches, the remainder of the bush can receive the necessary nutrients to bloom beautifully. Such products and services may have a legacy within the organization or be a favorite of some leader, but culling them quickly will add value to the remainder of the organization.

Keys to Your Insanity Check

Once you commit to an insanity check, there are several critical factors to remember as you move forward.

- **Build momentum.**

  The change initiatives you have started may take time to gain momentum before you actually see visible progress. You're laying the groundwork for improvement, building a foundation, and driving beliefs and values that will spill over into behavioral changes. You may be personally impatient, or stakeholders may be pushing you for quick results. But make sure your plan is solid and you're on track in following it. Stopping or pausing will undermine your energy, and you'll almost literally have to start over. So keep pushing and build momentum, your goal is in sight.

- **Pull the lever.**

  Identify the critical lever for change and focus on it. This critical lever is at the center of the problem and supports and reinforces what is not working. Like a house of cards, if you pull that lever, everything it supports will collapse, and that may be a good thing. Pulling the lever may require repositioning your team, changing your structure, developing a different strategy, or shifting your own leadership style.

- **Manage time.**

  Time is one of the most valuable resources you have, so use it wisely. Rather than succumb to the many demands on your time, control how you spend it by prioritizing those activities that add value to what you're trying to accomplish. I admit I can get caught up reading business books and articles that are interesting, yet aren't necessarily relevant to the project I'm working on, so I must refocus myself as well. Determine what activities add the most value, find the ones that are really drivers of significant change, and adjust your time accordingly.

Remember... working harder on a bad plan doesn't make the plan good. Doing the right thing at the wrong time won't achieve the desired results. Smart moves at the right time are key to reaching your goals and meeting your objective.

7. YOUR INNER CIRCLE
Building Your Leadership Team

"You will never outperform your inner circle."

—JOHN WOODEN, LEGENDARY HEAD COACH FOR THE
UNIVERSITY OF CALIFORNIA, LOS ANGELES, FROM 1948 TO 1975

Imagine that you want to move 4,000 pounds of metal, plastic, rubber, and fiber from your home to your office. In other words, you want to drive your car to work. The primary mechanism of movement you will need is a set of wheels. Since its invention more than 6,000 years ago, this basic tool has facilitated the transportation of objects across the world. The original design of the wheel was a solid frame until the discovery of spokes, which made it lighter, faster, and thus easier to use. While its design and aesthetics have evolved, the simplicity of the wheel's use has remained the same: it provides mobility and progress.

As a leader, imagine yourself as the central hub in a wheel. The rim forms a circle around your leadership team; it defines your inner circle. Your ability to move forward with your initiatives is dependent upon the strength and structural reliability of the spokes to which you're connected. These spokes must be strong and firmly attached to both the hub and the outer rim. Others see you as a unit, whose parts function effectively to the degree they are united. Because you're only as strong as your weakest link, it's important to build and strengthen your inner circle.

The Spokes of Leadership

Think about these five key qualities you need in your "spokes" to support a strong wheel.

1. **Alignment** *around vision, mission, shared goals, and objectives*

   These are the core philosophies of your "why," which according to Simon Sinek, is the purpose, cause, or belief that inspires you and your organization to do what you do. Involve your inner circle in discussions around the direction of your organization. They must fully understand each piece of the puzzle to see the big picture. Ensure the channels of communication are open for debate, respectful disagreement, and continual dialogue to make certain everyone is aligned. The point is, if there is disagreement around the vision and mission, it's best to hash it out in the open rather than let it fester in the background. Such dissent will act like a cancer and undermine your plans.

2. **Teamwork** *and collaboration, with everyone bringing complementary skills to the table*

   The Cleveland Cavaliers and the Golden State Warriors have met for the NBA playoffs for four consecutive years, from 2015 to 2018. But it's not just LeBron James of the Cavaliers or Steph Curry of the Warriors who will play. The ENTIRE team on each side must play. Each man must perform according to his position and work with his teammates to effectively win. As talented and critical as LeBron or Steph are to their respective team's success, they still can't win the games and the championship by themselves. So why do some leaders think they can play their role and everyone else's too? As the hub, you act as the coach or captain of the team. It all comes together around you, but every person must excel at and perform their assigned function.

3. **Integrity** *and standards of trust that hold everyone accountable*

   If the structural integrity of one of the spokes is below the

71

minimum design quality, it will break, damaging the entire system of the wheel. These same structural boundaries apply to behaviors in your inner circle. As the leader, you must model acceptable behaviors and clearly identify those which are improper. This includes clarifying ethical and moral values as well as daily behavioral norms. And your team must know that anyone who violates these standards will be dealt with in an appropriate way. Lack of trust in any of these areas weakens the fabric of the team.

4. **Culture** *clearly defined to ensure fit*
   When people are considering a new position, the first thing they want to understand is the culture of the organization so they can determine whether they fit. Do leaders communicate effectively? How are decisions made? How do they differentiate between simply good and really great employees? What do people like and dislike about working there? Purposefully discuss, define, and develop the culture of your inner circle. As you're considering candidates to join your team, include the members of your inner circle in the interview process to ensure their ability to work well together.

5. **Development** *and nurturing the growth of your inner circle*
   Just like a wheel needs to be maintained and the tire surrounding it must be inflated properly, your inner circle needs maintenance and care. You must nurture its growth and development, not only for succession planning but for the personal and professional development of its members. Watch for signs of weakness and take swift action to shore it up. Leverage strengths and talk about opportunities for development. You may need to invest in a coach, find a mentor, or provide a key experience or developmental assignment for your inner circle.

All of these spokes are also surrounded by the assumption that the team members have the technical capabilities to perform their roles. That's the basic price of consideration for entry into your inner circle. But skill and experience without the ability to function as a unit will stymie progress and negatively impact your business results. Similarly, if the wheel isn't structurally sound, it will collapse under the weight of the load it's carrying. You must, therefore, take the time to examine the spokes in your wheel and maintain them.

Who makes up your inner circle? Are your members contributing to your wheel's strength?

8. WHAT DOES YOUR CULTURE LOOK LIKE?
The Value of a Closer Look

*"Be very specific about behavior,
how it's impacting your problem and the
future state of the behavior you want to see."*

—EDGAR SCHEIN, FORMER PROFESSOR AT THE MIT SLOAN
SCHOOL OF MANAGEMENT, AUTHOR, AND FAMOUS
FOR HIS WORK ON ORGANIZATIONAL CULTURE

The house my husband and I live in is on a corner, and almost every summer day as part of my morning exercise I walk down the side street of our home. The sun is still rising. The dew hasn't yet vanished from the grass. Everything looks fresh and green. The bushes that we so carefully planted around the perimeter of our home several years ago have grown substantially since the landscaping service gave them their spring trim. As each day goes by, I realize that some parts of those shrubs are REALLY growing out, and maybe it's time for a midsummer trim earlier than we anticipated.

So one morning after my exercise, I casually grabbed a big, paper yard refuse bag from the garage, along with my favorite cutting tools, and meandered over to the two or three bushes that from a distance seemed to need special attention. Once I got close to them, I saw that the problem wasn't so much with the original bushes we planted as it was with other wild greenery growing up in the middle of them. I began clipping away at the branches until I could finally see the base of those stalks and move in with my more precise and sharp tool to cut them off just above the ground. That's as close as I could get, given that the roots seemed to be intertwined. Once I got all the wild, weedlike brush removed, I realized that the original bush was only half as full. The weed took up so much space that it prevented the original bush from growing. As my one bag filled up quicker than anticipated, I began to recognize the enormity of the issue. There weren't just two or three bushes that needed attention, there were about EIGHT!

That's when I realized the landscaping service just cut the bushes *back* versus cutting *out* the greenery that wasn't supposed to be there in the first place. If I or my husband had paid more attention to the job that needed to be done, or how the bushes were developing, maybe we could have caught this earlier. Instead, now we needed to surgically remove the vegetation that didn't belong there in order to nurture the greenery that was consistent with our original intent. This created more work for us and lost growth for the plants themselves.

A Picture of Your Culture

Given my passion for leadership, I began to think about the lesson to be learned for organizations. Leaders who talk about the culture and the behaviors they want in their organizations but fail to follow through and ensure everyone knows what to do and how to do it are likely to get inconsistent results. They may be too distant from the middle and lower layers of their team and fail to describe and model the behaviors of success. They may never stop to verify results, talk with the team, or gain feedback and input from others. This neglect leads to manifestation of undesirable behaviors in their organizations.

A colleague recently told me about a manufacturing company with a relatively long product development cycle. While the entry-level engineers would recognize issues in the products they were asked to develop, the culture didn't encourage or reward open communication and identification of potential problems, and they learned to simply kept quiet. These issues were passed along for several years, until they were much bigger and resulted in product launch delays and significant cost overruns that tarnished their brand image. Their "weeds" had a very costly consequence.

The same results occur in our professional and personal lives, where seemingly small and unchecked negative behaviors blossom until they derail careers or ruin relationships. The culture of a company or personality of an individual must be carefully cultivated, based on desired outcomes that support the purpose of the organization.

Build an Aligned Culture

Culture is observable in the beliefs, behaviors, knowledge, experiences, and values of an organization and the individuals in it. So how can leaders redirect their focus to build a culture that aligns with the desired results of the company?

1. **Frame the desired environment.**
   Do you want an organization that encourages associates to come up with creative ideas, promotes wellness, or values teaming with members of diverse functional groups? What behaviors contribute to the overall performance of the company?

2. **Identify the behaviors and policies to be changed.**
   What embedded processes, norms, and actions hinder the desired state? Most importantly, which leaders (and their behaviors) impede that development? In discussing this issue, everything should be "put on the table" for review and consideration.

3. **Determine the daily habits to get there.**
   Once you identify what's wrong, replace it with what's right. None of us get rid of bad habits without first focusing on good replacement habits. The leadership team should model behaviors and implement processes and systems to support the desired culture.

4. **Reward and reinforce.**

Identify reward mechanisms in the process, along with a means to catch deviations early on. Unwanted behaviors are generally deeply rooted, so it's necessary to proactively dig in and stop them from spreading. You'll need close and continual monitoring and pruning to develop your desired culture.

These high-level steps obviously require a significant amount of engagement and time on the part of the leadership team, and frequently are best addressed by collaborating with culture change experts. However, the return on investment is multiplied in providing exponentially superior business outcomes. Ultimately, the desire to shift to a more beneficial culture must be greater than the discomfort of going through the change process and weeding out the negative behaviors, beliefs, experiences, and values.

What does your culture look like?

9. LET IT GO
Making Room for New Opportunities

"Consumers are beginning in a very real sense to own our brands and participate in their creation...We need to begin to learn to let go."

—A. G. LAFLEY, CHAIRMAN, PRESIDENT AND CEO, PROCTOR AND GAMBLE

Technology changes and times change, but sometimes it's hard to let go of what was once a good thing.

Several years ago, in a fury of "decluttering," I decided to remove the perfectly good CD/cassette tape stereo from my office bookshelf and give it to a charity. Truthfully, I hadn't even used it in years. It was just taking up space that could be better occupied by something more relevant. Then, in another burst of energy and insight, I gathered up all the old cassette tapes stored away (I don't even remember why), the CD/DVD teaching packages that were regularly dusted but otherwise ignored, and gave them all away to The Salvation Army. I'll admit I had a moment of sentimentality. The information and music shared via these mediums was still good, but the method and technology by which they were delivered no longer met my needs.

Shifting Trends

Technology is shifting in other venues as well. Sporting events that were traditionally filmed from above via blimps are now being covered by drones, thereby capturing great angles and shots never before seen. This makes watching such games all the more enjoyable for sports enthusiasts.

The owner of Columbia House, a formerly well-known mail order music giant, filed for Chapter 11 bankruptcy protection in 2015. The company acknowledged that annual revenue from its membership-based sales of CDs and DVDs had been dropping over the past 20 years, from a high of $1.4 billion to just $17 million.

Earnings and ratings continue to decline as more and more consumers are dropping traditional cable TV packages and "cutting the cord," switching to streaming media services such as Netflix. Technology is enabling far greater consumption of media, as we can now watch what we want when we want, and how we want it.

Where Does That Leave Us in the Business Realm?

Remember that corporations are simply collections of people like you and me. We bring our traditions, preferences, approaches, and personal styles to our individual roles, which are then somehow integrated into the organizational culture. Many companies have failed to adopt new methodologies, often because their people rely too much on what worked in the past. They continue to utilize company resources to support products, processes, and initiatives whose "expiration date" has passed.

Instead, each organization should conduct an annual review of what they should stop doing. Where are they holding on to old ways of doing things just because they're familiar? Where are they getting stuck in the past because they used to make money that way? Where do they need to cut the cord, make a clean break, sweep out the dregs, and provide clean space to innovate on new approaches?

Obviously, this isn't easy, because there are people who have a vested interest in some of these outdated, expired products, processes, and services. Why not start the conversation by conducting an analysis of the Strengths, Weaknesses, Opportunities, and Threats (SWOT) of various functions of your business. Evaluate the financial, client, and public relations implications, and focus on the leading edge of innovation in that space.

What Do You Let Go of and How Do You Replace It?

There are five strategic areas where we typically find it difficult to "let go" and embrace change.

1. *A business process that's cumbersome and doesn't serve your client's needs*

   This might include processes to provide customer support, tracking consumer preferences, monitoring equipment failure rates to diagnose problems, or managing your supply chain. If it's been in place for a long time, or the technology supporting it has changed, now is the time to evaluate whether it's still working or determine what would work better. How can you save time and money? How can you empower individuals more in the process? How can you reevaluate the fundamental assumptions upon which it is based and decide if they will be relevant in the next three years? If not, how can you move ahead of the curve?

2. *A product line that has been experiencing lagging sales or doesn't meet future customer requirements*

   Maybe there's a small but loyal following, but is that worth the ongoing cost of marketing, manufacturing, reengineering, and quality control? How can you transition the client base to a new and improved product that can be enjoyed by a broader cross section of the market—one that will exceed their expectations and delight them?

3. **Technology that doesn't deliver on the desired user experience**

Customers shouldn't equate your company with outmoded equipment or machinery, or systems that are slow to respond. Explore your options to leverage new technology in a lower-cost way. Engage stakeholders to encourage their acceptance of the upcoming changes. And most importantly, sit with your customers to understand their perspective on working with your organization so that you can address major issues.

4. **Strategies that simply aren't working or producing the desired results**

A November 2018 CNN article referenced Burger King's announcement of their new strategy, Burger King of Tomorrow, which focused on updating their stores with open kitchens, digital menu boards, double drive-through lanes, and more. This modernization plan was a replacement of their prior "gimmicky" marketing strategies of providing different food options and packaging to bring traffic into the stores, which didn't produce the desired results.[17] The company is, however, playing catch-up with its competitors, who already had similar plans well underway. No matter the amount of resources poured into developing a strategy, there's a point in time to recognize failure and cut your losses. In this situation, Burger King decided it was better served by focusing a new direction.

5. **A job that no longer aligns with your career goals, developing interests, or professional values**

Over the past three decades of coaching and developing employees, I've seen far too many people who stay in a job because it's comfortable. Not only has the job long ceased to align with their interests, they are not adding great value to their employers. We do our best work when we're engaged and passionate about what we do. This may mean leaving a so-called "safe" space (because you know the culture and it pays the bills) to venture into a new environment with better opportunities.

81

Cleaning out the old creates the psychological and physical space for innovation and transformation. It gets your brain out of focusing on what used to be and allows you to imagine things on a new level. As a leader, don't permit your team to cling to the past. This blocks their ability to embrace the future. Instead, help them to make room for new opportunities by driving and managing change. This is the tipping point for the overall health and growth of the organization.

17. Danielle Wiener-Bronner, "How Burger King Fell Behind," CNN Business, November 13, 2018, https://www.cnn.com/2018/11/13/business/burger-king-strategy/index.html.

10. THE MIGHTY ONES
From Hubris to Humility

"Hubris can lead to making brash commitments for more and more and more. And then one day, just when you've elevated expectations too far, you fall. Hard."

—JIM COLLINS, AUTHOR, CONSULTANT, AND LECTURER
ON THE SUBJECT OF BUSINESS MANAGEMENT
AND COMPANY SUSTAINABILITY AND GROWTH

The applause was deafening. The congratulations overwhelmed your email box. The press clippings were glowing. Everyone was buzzing because your recent product launch was successful. Last quarter's earnings beat even the analysts' predictions. The company's stock price was up 15 percent, operating costs were down, and sales volumes were number one in the industry.

So how do you follow that act? All of this excitement doesn't build a platform upon which to rest. Instead, it forms a higher bar than the last one, over which you must hurdle. After all, the stockholders expect more earnings, customers expect better products, and employees expect more bonuses and career opportunity. And so it goes.

How do you manage all of these expectations for continuous improvement against the best strategy for the company's growth?

How do you compete for market dominance without succumbing to market vulnerabilities? This is the pivotal point. The choices you make will become either a stepping stone to greater victory or the rock that trips up your company, your team, or your own leadership success.

Companies and people don't automatically enter a "safe" zone when they reach a measure of accomplishment. But in some cases their behavior suggests they think their momentum can't be stopped. You've heard the saying "the higher you climb, the harder you fall"? While that doesn't necessarily have to be true, in the midst of success it's important to remain grounded, like holding onto a guardrail.

Best-selling author Jim Collins explains what's behind the failure of once top companies. In his book, *How the Mighty Fall: And Why Some Companies Never Give In*, he highlights five stages.[18]

1. **Hubris born of success**

   Here an organization or team exhibits extreme pride and arrogance based on past accomplishments.

2. **Undisciplined pursuit of more**

   Companies in this stage overreach, become obsessed with growth, and fail to manage the process and pace effectively, ultimately undermining their long-term value.

3. **Denial of risk and peril**

   By this stage, companies are so caught up in successes they become blind to the possibilities of failure.

4. **Grasping for salvation**

   This is the moment where the company's decisions lead to new life or certain death.

5. **Capitulation to irrelevance or death**

   At this point, organizations are spiraling out of control and either give in to certain death or shrink into irrelevance.

Collins describes a culture that is focused on increasing greed and self-promotion, where leaders literally feel they *own* their customers. Their "might" is defined by their ability to amass ever greater profits. A situation which, over time, becomes unsustainable. A different definition of "might" can be defined as an organization's ability to effectively *serve* and engage their customers. This emanates from a culture focused on promoting and giving to others; a culture of humility. Here are a few tips from my playbook to support that approach:

■ **Build a culture of service.**

Think of others' needs first. Encourage a *giving* mentality—where long-term relationships, integrity, and quality products or services are most meaningful—instead of a *getting* mentality where there's constant pressure on the customer to take actions that support your profits.

■ **Find your truth teller.**

Unfortunately, some leaders surround themselves with people who will tell them what they want to hear. Or they don't create a culture where their team feels comfortable fully informing them about business issues. Make sure you surround yourself with people who are encouraged and willing to speak up and say the difficult things or raise questions that may be contrary to the prevailing direction.

■ **Know the value you add.**

Keep the focus on the value you provide to your customers and the "why" of your organization. Know what differentiates you from your competition. Know why your customers are attracted to your product or service. Communicate regularly with them to stay in tune with and respond to their needs. Find ways to improve or innovate, and don't hesitate to shift gears when you see the market changing. Be quick to shed those activities that aren't value added in serving them.

- **Exhibit learning leadership.**
  Only when the leader of the team demonstrates a continual desire to learn, admits faults and deficiencies, and seeks input from the entire team and people outside the company will others in the organization follow suit.

Note that these recommendations have nothing to do with functional or technical skills. You can hire individuals on your team to fulfill those roles. This has everything to do with pure leadership—influencing others to move forward in the right direction based on the right decisions. These are critical steps in building a "mighty" organization and becoming a "mighty" leader.

18. Jim Collins, "Five Stages of Decline" in *How the Mighty Fall: And Why Some Companies Never Give In*, (New York: Collins Business Essentials, an imprint of HarperCollins *Publishers*, 2009).

LEADERSHIP PERSPECTIVE REFLECTIONS

With the exponential rate of change among industries in the context of customer needs, technological innovation, government regulation, and pressure for greater social responsibility, leaders must be pro-active in shifting their perspectives on how they address business challenges. Equally important, employees have shifting expectations of how they want to contribute to their companies and use their capabilities and skill sets. This challenges leaders to reflect on their foundational viewpoints that guide their decisions.

Reflect further on these **Leadership Perspective** topics:

◆ How is your perspective impacting your ability to lead effectively?

◆ What risks are you managing in your role and career, and how do you effectively manage them?

◆ How can you address the urgent issues, yet shift more of your organization's attention to the important issues you need to face?

◆ How can you integrate the process of gaining new perspectives into your daily or weekly routine?

◆ Who among your work colleagues provides the balance in different perspective you need to fully evaluate situations?

◆ What leadership activities do you keep repeating that aren't generating the results you need?

◆ Who's in your inner circle? And how have they earned the right to be there?

◆ When was the last time you closely examined your organization's culture to determine if it really aligns with your objectives?

◆ What are you holding onto that no longer serves a valid purpose for you and your organization?

◆ How can you foster a culture of humility within your organization?

Step 3.

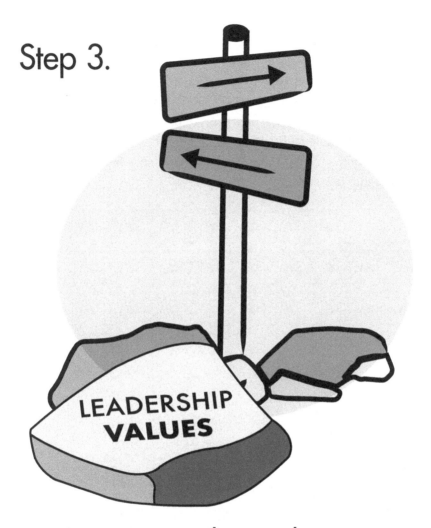

LEADERSHIP **VALUES**

Principles and
standards that support
constructive leadership

The next set of articles is about Leadership **Values.** These are principles and standards to support constructive leadership. They are foundational beliefs about what is important as you lead. This is another opportunity to dig deep and think about the underlying reasons as to why you do what you do. You may find that some of your values have a solid base while others shift with the wind. They may vary according to what seems politically expedient at the moment and you might not be able to readily explain why they are critical. This is an opportunity to ensure you've identified your core beliefs that guide your leadership behaviors.

1. FAITH@WORK
A Pathway to Success

"Faith is like Wi-Fi, it's invisible but has the power to connect you to what you need."

—UNKNOWN

D oes faith have a place at work? CEOs at some major corporations think so.

John Tyson, chairman of Tyson Foods, doesn't believe that faith needs to be checked at the door when you come to work. He believes "faith is just an ongoing evolution, trying to understand what faith in the marketplace looks like, giving people permission to live their faith seven days a week...If people can talk about the football game on Monday, why can't they talk about their faith?" Tyson Foods employs chaplains to provide support to employees of all faiths, whether Christian, Jewish, or Muslim.[19]

Conrad Hilton, founder of Hilton Hotels, had a deep devotion to God that permeated his business decisions and personal life. Upon

91

his death, he left most of his fortune to a Catholic charity, with the statement that "There is a natural law, a divine law, that obliges you and me to relieve the suffering, the distressed, and the destitute."[20]

Do Won and **Jin Sook Chang** are cofounders and owners of the popular fashion brand Forever 21. As professed Christians, they share that God told them to open the store, and they continue to attend church every morning. Mr. Chang keeps a Bible open on his desk and has placed the scripture John 3:16 on the bottom of every store bag as a statement of faith.[21]

What Is Faith?

Faith is confidently trusting that something will happen, particularly when we don't yet understand how it's possible. Often evoking a spiritual attitude, faith is associated with a belief in a higher power, such as God. To achieve an objective, faith requires some action based on your belief.

One of my favorite examples of faith comes from the movie *Indiana Jones and the Last Crusade*. At the climax of the movie, Indiana (played by Harrison Ford) must save his father's life by quickly finding the Holy Grail. He comes to the edge of a cliff and, according to his map, he must somehow get across a bottomless chasm to the side of the neighboring cliff. There's no visible means to cross it and nowhere else to go, but the map has proven true up to this point. Indiana takes a deep breath, then lifts one foot and steps forward, muttering that he's taking a "leap of faith." His sigh of relief is palpable when he finds that a span of rock has appeared before him, bridging the distance across the deep void. His belief in the origin of the map was the basis for exercising faith that his steps were correct. In a similar manner, your experience with the maker of your "map" is your basis for exercising faith.

Can You Really Bring Faith to Work?

The 2014 U.S. Religious Landscape Study by the Pew Research Center[22] reports that 70 percent of the population claims some affiliation with Christian religions (Protestant, Catholic, etc.), while almost 6 percent identify with a non-Christian faith (i.e., Jewish,

Muslim), and another 22 percent report no religious affiliation. These numbers indicate that a high percentage of employees bring some measure of faith into the workplace. Yet, like politics, it is an often avoided or delicately approached topic for fear of offending or being accused of proselytizing others.

As companies seek to engage and retain employees, and talk about "bringing your whole self to work," there may be a benefit in opening up an appropriate dialogue about faith at work. In doing so, it's vital for leaders to set the tone of mutual respect and openness to various perspectives.

As a leader for many years in corporate America, I brought my faith to work every day. It was rarely a topic of explicit conversation, but it was ever present in my thoughts and approach. Most important-ly, it provided me with the ability to view situations not as they *were*, but as they *could be*, with God powerfully working through me and my team to achieve appropriate goals. I felt I was given each assignment to accomplish His purpose in my environment.

I often prayed on my way to work and while walking to meet-ings. This took my focus off my own capabilities and placed it instead on God's ability to intervene in every aspect of my work life. I memorized scriptures that helped me to concentrate on how God would guide me in a variety of situations. Thus, instead of overreacting emotionally when things didn't go as planned, this gave me a new level of peace. Yes, there were times when my anxiety would increase as a result of a particular issue, but that was also a sign I needed to take a deep breath and focus on the only power I knew who could guide me through it.

I've found that leaders who exercise faith at work tend to follow four strategies for success.

1. They **listen.**
   They have a relationship with God and know how to hear His voice speaking to them. Specifically, they hear what God is saying about their work, ideas on how to complete it, and insights and wisdom on how to approach it. They also aren't afraid to dream big.

2. They **obey.**

These leaders put their faith into action, even when it doesn't appear to make sense. They aren't afraid of what others will think. They trust the process and are more comfortable seeing just the next step ahead, instead of the complete pathway.

3. They **believe.**

God is really working in and through these faith-filled leaders, and He has a bigger plan than they can imagine. They've seen it work before and know it can happen again. So they're not surprised when unexpected things happen, impossibilities become possibilities, and paradigms shift.

4. They **receive.**

Leaders who exercise their faith at work remain open to miracles from God, which are manifested in tangible business results and achievements.

Do you bring your faith to work? If so, how does it show up as an asset in your workplace?

19. Justin Rohrlich, "Religious CEOs: Tyson Foods' John Tyson," Minyanville Media, May 19, 2010.

20. Holly Lebowitz Rossi, "7 CEOs with Notably Devout Religious Beliefs," *Fortune*, November 11, 2014, http://fortune.com/2014/11/11/7-ceos-with-notably-devout-religious-beliefs/.

21. Eva Wiseman, "The Gospel According to Forever 21," *The Guardian*, July 16, 2011, https://www.theguardian.com/lifeandstyle/2011/jul/17/forever-21-fast-fashion-america.

22. "Religious Landscape Study," Pew Research Center, May 12, 2015, http://www.pewforum.org/religious-landscape-study/.

2. FEAR@WORK
Change the Climate

"Good leadership requires you to surround yourself with people of diverse perspectives who can disagree with you without fear of retaliation."

—DORIS KEARNS GOODWIN, PRESIDENTIAL
BIOGRAPHER AND HISTORIAN

Lucas finished his workweek and slowly drove home. This was the most frustrating week in the three months since he assumed his new role as president of the packaged goods business unit of his company. He had such high hopes when he accepted the promotion from the durable goods business unit. He didn't know many of the leaders on this new team, but he was impressed from a distance with their metrics and profitability. Now that he had led the team long enough to understand the secret to their success, he found it was a fragile environment, complete with a few shady operating practices.

One of the most frustrating findings was that it was difficult for Lucas to build relationships with his employees. He was used to frequent interactions, listening to employees' ideas and concerns, being transparent with them about the state of the business and why decisions were made, and engaging in discussions on the pros and cons of various business strategies. Lucas preferred an energetic environment where he and other leaders emphasized providing what employees needed to perform well on their jobs. Like an inverted pyramid with the leaders on the bottom, he believed his leadership role was to support his employees, not them working to support him.

Instead, Lucas found a quiet atmosphere in which everyone was always "heads down," avoiding eye contact. When he wandered through various areas of the building, it was difficult to engage employees in conversation. His questions about the projects they were working on were met with respectful but terse responses. He also recognized that employees weren't taking the initiative to come up with solutions to problems. They seemed to direct anything controversial to the leadership team for resolution. Finally, at his All Team meeting today, when he opened up the floor for questions, no one said a thing. Even the employees who used the private app to submit questions kept them very high level and straightforward.

As Lucas drove home in the bumper-to-bumper traffic, he finally pinpointed the issue with his team: There was a culture of fear among the employees. Fear was paralyzing them and keeping them from stretching and experimenting with new ideas. They were indecisive in their quest to figure out what their leaders wanted to hear or wanted them to do because they were afraid of the repercussions of a wrong decision. Lucas had heard of a few occasions where his direct reports responded negatively and seemingly irrationally to employees' questions and concerns. Thus, diverse viewpoints on achieving organizational objectives were not being brought forward and employee attrition in packaged goods was the highest among all the business units in the company.

Lucas knew this was serious. His employees' internal insecurities ("Am I meeting others' expectations in how I'm performing in my role?") were colliding with external uncertainties. ("Will I become a victim of how the environment is shifting around me?") Their preoccupation with issues of job security, job performance, leadership changes, industry direction, and business capability was distracting them from doing their best work. He needed to find a way to build an environment of trust and avoid fertilizing any seeds of fear.

As Lucas reflected on his past experiences, he knew trust had to be built on relationships (knowing people well), transparency (understanding the underlying motives of your colleagues and leaders), and predictability (being able to correctly anticipate behavior). He had to identify his leadership team's key behaviors that were fueling fear among the employees and teach those leaders new behaviors. But how could Lucas accomplish his goal?

Changing the Climate

Lucas's experience is not unusual. Toxic leaders, like those in his organization, create widespread fear among employees. Similar to sickness, that fear causes them to shut down and do just enough to get by. Fear manifests in low employee engagement scores, lack of collaboration between teams, and high attrition. To change the climate, you must start with the leaders. They are the ones who set the tone, demonstrate behaviors, and model values for employees. More than just giving lip service to it, aligning leaders' behaviors communicates the important actions for employees to model. To build trust and root out sources of fear in their organization, Lucas and his leaders needed to implement several key strategies:

■ **Determine predictability.**
   Sure, it's impossible to predict your organization's future in this Volatile, Uncertain, Complex, and Ambiguous (VUCA) environment where there are so many influences beyond your control. But what you can predict is how your organization responds to them. It's called culture, and every one of your employees should understand the behaviors and values that are the norm and are expected of them. Employees should have a strong sense of knowing how the

organization will react to whatever situation occurs—that they will be treated with respect, communications will be transparent, hard work will be appreciated, and smart work will be recognized.

■ **Take responsibility.**
Leaders who don't make any mistakes either aren't human or aren't trying to do anything worthwhile. Mistakes will happen. The question is, how will you handle them? Recognize and correct a mistake quickly, admit your role in it, don't blame or berate others, help them to learn from it, and move on. If employees believe that leaders will respond irrationally or negatively to mistakes, they will be careful not to take any risks. And the few who are willing to take risks will be considered the "golden" ones, who know they are highly valued and will be supported in the process. Failure to identify with mistakes stifles creativity and innovation. Instead, leaders should transparently share their own mistakes and offer what they've learned from them.

■ **Be genuine and authentic in your communications.**
Avoid leadership communications to employees that say one thing while everyone knows the leaders intend and will do something else. Those emails may sound good, but they don't authentically represent what's happening in the organization. Share your heart with your team, don't just say what you think they need to hear. Acknowledge their strengths, along with the areas where team members need to grow.

■ **Be clear and consistent on your boundaries of acceptable behavior.**
Employees should know that when there's a question of improper behavior, there will be a fair investigation. Make a positive example of employees who comply with government regulations or laws, as well as company policies, ethics, and morals. Don't promote a culture of "don't ask, don't tell," or tacit ignorance of such violations

emanating from senior leaders, where employees feel caught between the proverbial "rock and a hard place" in knowing what to do.

- **Acknowledge the impact of media.**
  These days, negative and incomplete media coverage of corporate issues has a tremendous impact on due process and outcomes. Companies feel compelled to make decisions based on public perception and social media outrage, which doesn't always reflect reality. In a small percentage of cases, this may unfairly impact some individuals. A proactive stance ensures everyone understands the importance of making decisions that build relationships and are in the best interests of the public, investors, clients, and employees. Likewise, it's also recognized that any behavior one wouldn't want magnified in the press should be avoided.

- **Invest in your employees' growth and development.**
  There is always a concern employees may take their newly gained knowledge and go work for your competitor. But if you engage them with challenging assignments, they may also stay and contribute to your business growth. Yet employee loyalty has long since moved from a vertical relationship with their employer (30-40 years at the same company) to a horizontal relationship with their functional colleagues (networking with peers via social media and professional organizations). Workers have seen too many friends and family members "downsized" and, therefore, realize they need to build competitive skills. Demonstrate an interest in how their future aligns with your organization's future to build trust and strong relationships.

A climate of fear doesn't fade quickly, it erodes over time by the repeated and purposeful behaviors of the leadership team. Change starts at the top, by ridding the C-suite of "fear based" actions and attitudes. As leaders model and reward the behaviors and values they desire, they set a clear expectation for others to follow.

3. LEADERSHIP DISCIPLINES FOR SUCCESS
Building a High-Functioning Team

*"Discipline is the bridge between
goals and accomplishment."*

—JIM ROHN, ENTREPRENEUR, AUTHOR,
AND MOTIVATIONAL SPEAKER

What disciplines do you practice to ensure your leadership success?

Leadership disciplines are controlled behaviors designed to accomplish specific objectives. They are determined based on the individual leader's personal style and skill sets, their roles and responsibilities, and the culture and needs of the organization where they function in a leadership capacity.

While leadership can be learned, it requires discipline to be effective. It requires identifying and establishing a pattern or system of behaviors, and then repeating those behaviors until they become habits ingrained in your routine.

The roles and responsibilities of a leader will vary based on the operating structure and size of their organization. The ability to effectively hold a leadership role in a Fortune 100 company, a family owned business, a midsized nonprofit, city government, or as a budding entrepreneur is different for each person. But the need for discipline is consistent across every setting.

One definition of leadership is *establishing a relationship with others to influence behaviors and accomplish a goal.* Thus, leadership discipline is significant, because no matter the size of the team, everyone is watching, and to some degree is imitating the leader. And the fact that everyone is watching the leader makes it important to model the right behaviors. These behaviors are determined by the results the leader wants to accomplish.

Building Discipline

Athletes provide a great example of the need for discipline. They come in all shapes and sizes, from little league superstars to multimillion-dollar professionals. But each has to learn the disciplines of their respective sport in order to improve their skill level and be competitive. Here are four key steps to this discipline.

1. **Repetition**

   Specific physical movements are necessary to excel in each position of every sport. Baseball pitchers have to learn how to throw at different speeds and trajectories, and with varying breaks on the pitch. All of this requires extensive practice and training. But over time, pitchers build muscle memory, such that it becomes almost automatic. They couple this with knowing exactly what pitch to use with each batter, depending on the batter's record and the status of the game.

   Similarly, leaders in specific industries, cultures, positions, and organizational challenges have to identify the right behavior to constantly repeat to get the results they intend. If they are consistent, the organization comes to expect and anticipate their behavior and responses. Too often, though, leaders make a short-term commitment to improve or change their behavior but fail to stick with it. This not only defeats the purpose, it erodes trust among their team about their commitment to the cause. Ultimately, whatever behavior the leader regularly exhibits is the behavior the team comes to expect, whether positive or negative.

2. **Playbook**

Every sports team has a playbook that lays out the routines necessary for them to perform and win. This is so that every team member understands their own role and responsibilities, and that of their teammates. And it specifically identifies the tactics and plays which are appropriate for various situations.

Every leader similarly needs clearly laid out roles and responsibilities for the people on their team, so that everyone understands what to expect. This is more than just job responsibilities; it includes decision-making rights, communication processes, business outcomes, conflict management strategies, and more.

3. **Supporting behaviors**

Well-disciplined athletes treat their bodies as their most valuable resource. They make sure they eat food that provides the right fuel and nutrition, exercise in a manner that builds the right muscle mass, get sufficient rest, and work to improve their mental focus so they have the mindset of a winner.

Similarly, good leaders understand what their bodies and minds require for optimal performance. This may mean learning how to best function when extensive travel across multiple time zones is necessary; managing during extreme work circumstances that include physical, mental, or emotional challenges; and finding their most creative and productive workspace.

4. **Self-control**

Successful athletes learn that discipline is necessary not only when practicing and playing, but 24/7. They must exhibit appropriate behaviors, establish personal boundaries, and prioritize their time.

Fair or not, someone is always watching, and the more successful the athlete, the greater the expectations others have of them.

Similarly, leaders are always "on." Employees who see leaders drink excessively at the bar after work, drive erratically, display rudeness to a waiter or waitress, or behave disrespectfully to a spouse will incorporate those pieces of information into their overall perception of the leader. And if that behavior is inconsistent with their workplace persona, it will negatively impact the leader's image.

Discipline and Trust

Disciplined leaders build trust with their employees. As these leaders display consistent behaviors over time, their employees develop a level of predictability in the expectations and responses of their leader. Employees understand the necessary behaviors for success by example and can model that same behavior. When the leaders' behaviors are positive, constructive, and collaborative, and when they reward similar behaviors in their direct reports who lead others, it embeds those values within the organization.

When leaders' behaviors are erratic or unpredictable, trust is eroded and employee stress increases. And when employees are stressed and uncertain about their leaders, productivity declines and costs increase.

Leadership discipline is key to building a high-functioning team, so everyone works together and focuses on results. That discipline is built on having faith in one's own capabilities, and on the importance of providing consistent and constructive leadership for the organization.

What disciplines do **you** practice to make your leadership successful?

4. PRIDES, HERDS, AND TEAMS
The Value of Working Together

"If you want to go fast, go alone.
If you want to go far, go together."

—AFRICAN PROVERB

How well can you accomplish your goals by working alone?
Scrolling through my newsfeed recently, I came across an intense video of animals fighting for survival in the African bush. In it, a herd of 20-30 buffaloes rounded the bend in the path, their hooves thundering on the well-worn, dusty ground as they approached their watering hole. Suddenly, they stopped in their tracks, the blowing dust settling around them. They stood face-to-face with a pride of lionesses, six or seven of them, hungry and looking for their next meal. The fact that one buffalo was more than twice their size was unimportant to the lionesses. These large mammals were typically prey

for the pride; which had hungry cubs and several male lions to feed. Their goal was to isolate one buffalo from the others, then pounce as a group, using their powerful jaws to deliver a decisive strike to the throat, thereby suffocating the animal.

The standoff began with each group eyeing the other. This was routine for the buffaloes, and they knew they had strength in numbers. Several buffaloes at the front of the herd took turns rushing forward a few yards to butt the lionesses, more of an offensive measure than trying to jump on them. The lionesses responded in kind—crouching, half pouncing, looking for an angle to get in between a lone buffalo and the rest of the herd.

The buffaloes could only survive by working as a team. Similarly, the pride of lionesses' only hope of obtaining dinner was to operate as a team. On this day, the buffaloes won; their supportive strategy worked. The lionesses were unsuccessful in separating the group, and the buffaloes made it safely to their watering hole.

Individual Thinking

What lesson can we learn from these animals, whose survival instincts are so sharp? That working alone, and taking the role of individual contributor to the extreme, isn't the optimal operating mode for accomplishing your goals. Individual contributors are typically described as employees who don't have anyone reporting to them, and who may be tasked to operate more independently based on their assignment, skill set, and initiative. But doing so makes them susceptible to three personas that, when present in teams, leave members vulnerable, falling prey to organizational dynamics that can lead to failure.

■ **The Loners, who say, "I can do it by myself."**
They can come up with the ideas, work on the project alone, and evaluate all the issues by themselves. Yet there's a degree of arrogance in thinking their skill set and intellect alone are sufficient to find the best solution to address a problem.

- **The Distracteds,** who say, "Wait, where did everyone go? I wasn't paying attention!"
  They don't focus on the team, but instead get caught up in their own activities. They don't tune into, care enough about, or sense the spirit of the group.

- **The Schemers,** who say, "I'm going the right way, you all should follow me."
  They come up with what they think is a better idea and want to lead the group, but they haven't sought buy-in to their strategy. Their motives are self-serving and they haven't earned the right to have followers.

Each of these behaviors can isolate individual team members in ways that hamper effectiveness, sever relationships, compromise results, and end in conflict. Team members operating in one of these personas don't value the richness of group ideas and input, they don't respect the combined energy of the team, and they don't appreciate the support of their fellow members.

Teams Win

Our best work happens in teams, when we depend on one another to polish ideas, work through problems, and ensure plans and execution strategies are aligned across the organization. This begins with developing relationships, understanding and valuing the strengths each person brings to the table, and building trust.

Ultimately, like the herd of buffaloes and the pride of lionesses, we must understand that there's strength in the whole. It's no different than a football team, where everyone must play their position in order to win. The wide receiver can't decide to run his own play, the fullback can't be distracted by the cheerleaders, and the cornerback can't pick a different goal.

Teams win when individuals can't. A group of *good* individual players can become *great* when working together. Think about who's on your team. How are you communicating with them and helping each other achieve a common goal? You must effectively shift roles as needed, support others, and stick together when the going gets tough to deliver results. Whether you work in a large organization or as a solopreneur, you must come together with a community of contributors who possess varied and important skills to accomplish your objectives.

This is your opportunity to evaluate whether you're behaving like an individual contributor or a member of a great and successful team.

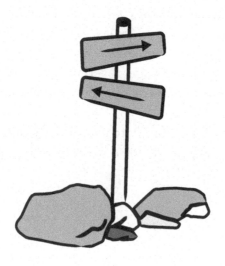

5. WHAT'S YOUR COMMUNICATION GOAL?
Compliance, Comprehension, or Change

*"Collaboration is a key part of the success of
any organization, executed through a clearly
defined vision and mission, and based on
transparency and constant communication."*

—DINESH PALIWAL, CEO OF HARMAN INTERNATIONAL INDUSTRIES

As leaders, we're constantly communicating to our stakeholders with strategic intent. The question becomes, how effective is your communication plan? This may sound simple, but amazingly, many leaders miss excellent opportunities to communicate with employees in ways that provide professional development. Explaining business decisions can enhance employees' understanding of priorities and engage them in driving sustained outcomes. When you're communicating with others, it's important to think about your goal to ensure your methodology, tone, and context will accomplish it.

A Case to Consider

It's the beginning of the fourth quarter of your fiscal year. Your company's revenues are not meeting projections. Sales forecasts in your industry show a year over year decline, and the cost of raw materials is going up. As CEO, you and your CFO meet with the leadership team and decide that spending must be slashed for the remainder of the year, and the following year's budget needs to be reduced by 10 percent. Because this is a critical issue, you want the organization to make this its first priority. You want the leaders to identify spending and budget reductions and submit updates to the finance team within a week. You consider three different approaches to communicating your request.

1. **Compliance**

   Expecting compliance is a common approach to communicating this all too frequent business ritual. You give the team direction on what they need to do, and they submit the desired response. While they know the company is in a tight position financially, this request is a transactional process; they have no buy-in to the decisions. You may achieve your goal, but with no lasting impact. Leaders will continue to justify expenditures and try to retain funding for otherwise not-so-important projects.

2. **Comprehension**

   A better approach is to explain the business financials to the employees in your organization. Help them to understand the cost drivers, industry trends, and allocation of resources. You and your leadership should review your business strategy and prioritize certain initiatives while putting others on hold. You share highlights of these deliberations to provide *insight* into how you arrived at your conclusions and the plans that are being put into place. Managers and employees will then be better equipped to make thoughtful decisions about where to identify spending and budget reductions.

109

3. Change

The best communication approach is one that drives change in the organization. There are underlying reasons for the financial condition of the company, both internal and external. More than an end-of-year exercise, this is an opportunity for a strategic review of the operating model, research and development investment, pricing strategy, and other business drivers. Instead of operating as a cost center, employees should understand how their work impacts the bottom line and regularly engage in reviews to improve effectiveness. In this way, employees have ownership in *influencing* the desired business outcomes.

The Flow

Good communication isn't a series of distinct events. It's an ongoing flow of interactions where leaders assess and understand the needs of others and continuously provide input to support those needs. Leaders who look at employees and think *they don't need to know this, I don't have time to explain it,* or *I don't know how to help them understand the leadership decision* will have shortsighted results. Employees can't drive better results when they don't comprehend the challenge.

Communication should be viewed as a developmental opportunity to help employees understand the broader context of their work, which will enable them to make better decisions. This interaction also serves as a basis for innovation and collaboration.

When driving major organizational changes, communication should be like the dripping of a faucet: frequent, consistent, and fluid. Employees who *frequently* hear from their leaders will feel more connected and aware of initiatives and decisions. Employees who *consistently* hear from their leaders learn to trust the process and the quality of information provided. And employees who *fluidly* hear from their leaders are more likely to engage in spontaneous interaction on tough but important questions around business decisions. This process enhances employee engagement and empowers team members to be more effective in their roles.

How are you communicating with your team?

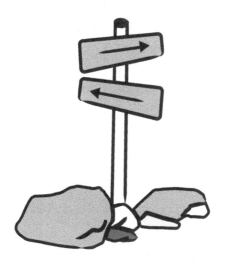

6. DARE TO BE DIFFERENT
5 Ways to Add Value to Others

*"Only those who dare to fail greatly
can ever achieve greatly."*

—ROBERT KENNEDY, FORMER U.S. ATTORNEY
GENERAL AND SENATOR

D *ares* are common among children at play. They dare each other
to do something outlandish or out of the norm that will certainly
be noticed by others. But these same children may grow up and lose
the nerve to take on some dares because the societal repercussions
are significantly greater as an adult.

Differences represent elements or traits which provide complementary components to create a fully functioning system. For
example, the human body is comprised of many different internal and
external parts, each with its own specific purpose, that follow the
brain's lead to perform smoothly. A symphony is comprised of many

different instruments, some with significant parts and others with smaller parts, each eliciting a beautiful sound when properly following the conductor and the music.

In the same way, we all bring a uniqueness to our team and organization. Whether an individual functions in seemingly important or more minor ways, we all are nonetheless vital to the success of the team. Therefore, failure to share our full value may result in the organization missing an opportunity for innovation, being unable to meet client needs, or overlooking costly design flaws. As leaders, it's essential to prioritize the growth and development of each team member's *differences* to draw out their value to the broader organization.

Five Dares

I had a stark reminder of the value of differences while watching the movie *Concussion*, starring Will Smith. It followed the true story of Dr. Bennet Omalu, a forensic pathologist who discovered a neurological deterioration similar to Alzheimer's disease in the brains of deceased professional football players. Dr. Omalu named this condition chronic traumatic encephalopathy (CTE) and published his findings in a medical journal. Faced with public rejection, he worked to raise consciousness about the long-term risks of football related head trauma.

After reviewing Dr. Omalu's struggle, it became evident that he *dared to be different* in five specific ways that reflected his value to his profession. These five specific dares are also relevant to the work of other leaders and change agents.

1. **Dare to be creative: Do something original, new, and different.**
   Dr. Omalu used different medical tools for his autopsies than other physicians did because those tools were more helpful in coming to the right conclusions. And while he had to follow proper medical protocol, he also used creativity in his approach by talking to his deceased patients (more on that in a minute), disposing of

his knives after each autopsy, and treating each result almost as a work of art. He had a deep respect for understanding the person's life as a means for understanding their death.

Your creative genius lies in the midst of a problem that irritates you, or an issue or idea that is constantly on your mind. As a leader, take the time to nurture creativity in each of your employees. Where possible, provide an opportunity for them to explore their capabilities and take on interesting projects.

2. **Dare to be caring: Pay attention to and be concerned about the needs of others.**

Dr. Omalu cared about his patients even though they were deceased. Before he started each autopsy, he would place his hand on the body, speak to the deceased by name, and ask the body to tell him what happened so that he could get to the root cause of why the person died.

There's a saying that when you show care and concern for your employees, they in turn will show care and concern for your customers. Your daily leadership decisions and policies send a clear signal to your team about how you value people. Your team members know if you're sincere. Instead of coming into work each day focusing on what YOU need, focus instead on what each member needs to be able to contribute fully, whether personally or professionally. This encourages members to perform at their best.

3. **Dare to be curious: Be eager to learn or know more.**

Dr. Omalu's curiosity to understand the reason behind the unexplained neurological condition led to a new diagnosis that has informed millions of people in their athletic pursuits and personal medical decisions. What's more amazing is that he paid tens of thousands of dollars out of his own pocket to reach this diagnosis, because his employer didn't have the funds, nor was it their policy to pay for this advanced research.

Curiosity is a precursor to learning; it's the driver and motivator. Though it's easy to be consumed with the daily challenges of leadership roles, it's important to take time to explore insights in related areas to stimulate thought processes and spur new ideas. A well-rounded team should include individuals who are curious about a variety of topics that can support your objectives. If your team knows that you reward and respect inquisitiveness, this gives them permission to ask more questions.

4. **Dare to be incorrect: Your values and decisions may not always align with the norms in your organization.**
    Dr. Omalu's findings weren't politically correct. In fact, they were professionally and politically threatening to some. He had to fight to get his work recognized, and at one point wondered if he had failed.

    At some time during your career, you will be faced with the choice of being politically correct versus doing what you believe to be appropriate given the situation. Deviating from the norm like this will be challenging. You're taking a risk to chart a new pathway, and you may find yourself reexamining your principles and values to ensure you know what you stand for. But the outcome of a risk of this nature may result in a leap ahead by adding value in solving a persistent problem or meeting a need.

5. **Dare to be committed: Obligate yourself to pursue your passions and purpose.**
    Dr. Omalu was committed to the pathology lab and his discoveries therein. Several years after his work was published, he received an offer to work in Washington, D.C., in a prestigious government health administrative position. He was told that if he accepted the position, he'd never have to work in the pathology lab again. After some thought, he turned down this chance for more recognition and compensation because he knew his first love was working in the lab. *That* was his purpose and passion in life.

When you know your purpose and passion, even when you have just a broad directional understanding of what it is, commit yourself to that direction. When you're operating in your purpose, it's not work, it's play. Too many individuals try to follow the popular path that may seemingly lead to greater recognition, power, money, etc., and fall short when it doesn't align with their true gifts.

Collaborative Differences

Remember that *daring to be different* doesn't mean operating independently of everyone else. Instead, there's a great obligation to collaborate and cooperate with others in related areas to collectively add value to your objective. In our earlier examples, the human brain or a symphony conductor functioned as a central controller, receiving inputs from and providing outputs to all parts of the system for it to work together. In the same way, leaders should ensure their organizational culture, structure, and communications processes receive inputs and provide outputs that recognize the roles and value of its members in reaching a common goal.

Dare to be different, be that central controller, and collaborate with others to benefit the entire organization.

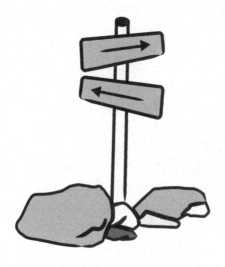

7. WHO OWNS YOU?
Taking Control of Your Future

*"It's not hard to make decisions once
you know what your values are."*

—ROY E. DISNEY, COFOUNDER, THE WALT DISNEY COMPANY

C EOs and business leaders are frequently confronted with the dichotomy of making decisions to ensure the long-term health of their companies while maximizing short-term profits. Their management roles compel them to lead the organization as if they are the owners, but in reality, these organizations are owned by and at the mercy of investors and customers who determine the value of their products and services.

In a 2016 survey conducted by *Fortune* magazine, 77 percent of CEOs said it would be easier to manage their companies if they were private.[23] This feedback comes amidst a climate of increasing numbers of activist investors who purchase a significant amount of company stock and then proceed to make recommendations to the board and company leadership on how they should run the business to increase its value. To be fair, all such suggestions are not bad, and some have led to considerably positive results in the bottom lines of these companies. But the CEO owners may find that their company's mission and purpose are no longer aligned with the direction in which others want them to move.

Customers also have a powerful voice in shaping corporate strategies and decisions. Pepsi worked hard over several years to reformulate its diet cola to remove aspartame, thereby meeting the needs of people who wanted to move away from artificial sweeteners. However, many other diehard Diet Pepsi drinkers didn't like the taste with the sucralose replacement and complained loudly. Pepsi then decided to return the old aspartame formula to market, selling both versions to meet the demands of all those customers. Oh, and did I mention that their sales volume slumped more than 10 percent during one of the quarters that the aspartame formula was off the market?

Ultimately, companies are at the mercy of and owned by their financial stakeholders. Whether you purchase shares of stock or a $5 product, you vote with your wallet on their future success. When strategic and principled decisions made by the board of directors and leadership team don't benefit the stakeholders, those decisions tend to become quickly challenged. While the senior leaders may hold critical positions in the company, the most important decisions are driven by clients and investors. Because if clients don't buy in to what you're selling, you won't be selling much for long. And if investors don't think you're a good growth prospect, they won't invest in your future.

Personal Ownership

Ownership in our personal lives mirrors the corporate experience. We pursue and accept positions based on our skill sets and a desired salary. We move up the career ladder based on positive feedback from others, in terms of our potential and added value. We take on different assignments at various companies because someone has said that we need to do it, even if it doesn't fit our dreams. Employers invest in us.

Clients decide they want what we're selling. And if we're not careful, we find ourselves in a position where we're no longer calling the shots on our own careers, our development, or our lives.

This is especially true for those in the spotlight, who are well-known or famous in their community, industry, or environment. Several examples in the Detroit area sports world include Calvin Johnson, all-time leading wide receiver for the Detroit Lions, and Pavel Datsyuk, star of the Red Wings hockey team. Johnson retired at age 30 after the 2015 season, walking away from a $16 million salary because he was simply tired of the wear and tear on his body. At 38, Datsyuk opted to walk away from $5.5 million in the middle of his contract to return to Russia and play his remaining few years in his home country. Their team owners, teammates, and fans—people who had emotional and financial investments in their careers—desperately wanted them to stay. But they each made a difficult decision to do what they knew was best for their families and them personally. They decided to own themselves.

Who Shapes YOUR Decisions?

The question for you and me is, what decisions are we making because of pressure from someone else who has invested time or money in us? It may be a mentor or sponsor, a spouse or parent, fans, friends, social media followers, customers, or financial investors in our business enterprises. Who has expectations of us that aren't aligned with our expectations of ourselves and our vision for the future? What will we lose by following *their* path of least resistance? What will we gain by following *our* path of greatest attraction? The goal at a personal level is to own our decisions, our work, and our future. We must avoid making decisions driven by short-term financial opportunity alone, and instead take the long-term view of how we can add value to others and fulfill our purpose. This means avoiding compromise with those who don't support our values and goals. We must choose carefully and wisely. Who owns YOU?

23. Geoff Colvin, "Take This Market and Shove It," *Fortune*, May 17, 2016, https://fortune.com/longform/going-private/.

8. INVEST IN YOURSELF
Your Leadership Portfolio

"Invest in yourself first. Expect nothing from no one and be willing to work for everything."

—TONY GASKINS, MOTIVATIONAL SPEAKER

Many years ago, there was a leader and queen of the country of Sheba by the name of Makeda.[24] As the ruler, she had many people and resources under her command. But rather than simply take pleasure in her obvious wealth, Makeda pondered how to better lead her people and handle the challenges of her country. Someone told her about another leader, named Solomon, who was the king of Israel. Solomon was known to be very wise and might be able to help her figure out how to manage some of the problems she was facing.

The queen must have been very concerned, frustrated, and maybe even desperate to find a better approach to her leadership issues, because she planned a major trip to visit him and talk about it.

She gathered the currency of her country in that day (many camels carrying spices, gold, and precious stones), and along with numerous servants traveled to meet with Solomon.

When Makeda arrived and sat down to talk with Solomon, the understanding she gained was overwhelming. The advance reports of his wisdom didn't even come close to matching her actual experience. Solomon not only understood her issues, he answered every question she had! His perspective and insight were so very great that he became a valuable mentor for her. Makeda observed Solomon's leadership style and capabilities, the engagement of his employees, his organizational culture, and the mission and focus of his team. Solomon's perceptiveness was so helpful to her in leading her country more effectively that she paid him with an abundance of the expensive resources she had brought.

While it's difficult to measure Makeda's resources in the context of her overall wealth, we do know it was the best of her country's possessions, because no one else ever gave Solomon such costly spices in so great a volume as she did. And in return, Solomon gave her all that she asked for.

Here was a leader, someone already accomplished enough to lead a large organization, who recognized the need and opportunity to learn more. She knew she had to continually improve her competencies to effectively build relationships, influence her team, and accomplish her organization's goals and objectives. She yearned to talk with someone else who understood leadership challenges and would support her in her initiatives. The queen's perspective on the resources she devoted to this opportunity was not about cost, but about making an investment in her own growth that would pay off in many ways in the long run.

Where Is Your Investment?

Popular business magazines dispense financial advice with a focus on how to make more money. They provide articles on all sorts of investments, tax reduction strategies, hot stock picks, and diversification tactics. But there are other important resource allocation decisions to make as well. The priority should be to invest in yourself, grow your own skills and abilities in pursuit of accomplishing your purpose and work, and strengthen your leadership. It's a safe investment to grow your capabilities, in that no one can take such growth away from you. Therefore, you should treat the development of your leadership portfolio similar to your financial portfolio by taking the following steps:

1. **Identify your personal and professional goals in the context of your life purpose.**
   That's the big "Why am I here?" question. Even as you're discovering your path and purpose, take stock of the capabilities you already have and those you need to gain to get to your sweet spot. This is a classic "learning gap" that applies to each of us at every level of our leadership journey. The bigger your goal and the wider the gap, the more resources (time and money) you'll need to devote to closing it.

2. **Invest in improving your leadership skills.**
   Commit to coaching, classes, books, leadership discussions, and practical application in your work environment. Seek out individuals who are experts in areas where you need to grow and learn from their experiences. Make a similar investment in your team to ensure there's alignment with individual and group goals, and support team members in building the right skills to meet your organizational objectives. While you may initially find the price to be greater than you anticipated, you'll soon learn the value of investing in the future.

3. **Diversify your leadership capabilities.**
   Ensure that your personal skills portfolio includes the generally required leadership traits (results orientation, strategic planning, decision-making, political savvy). Also be certain it includes the newer, critical leadership skills required to be competitive in today's fast-moving economy, such as driving innovation, leading

change, instilling creativity, exhibiting transparency, and displaying vulnerablilty.

Make a commitment to your personal leadership development in a
way that will benefit others. Make an investment in strategies that will
drive growth and outcomes for success.

If a queen can make this important investment, so can you.

24. Stefan Andrews, "The Elusive Queen of Sheba—Who Was She Really?," *The Vintage News*, March 9, 2019, https://www.thevintagenews.com/2019/03/09/queen-of-sheba/.

LEADERSHIP VALUES REFLECTIONS

When have you neglected to stand up for what you believed in because it represented a point of view that was different from the majority population in your organization? Has an idea ever come to your mind that you dismissed because it was out of the norm? Were you afraid to pitch it to the executive committee, or even share it with anyone because it might be viewed as too risky? Have you ever neglected to take a leap of faith because it was so counter to anything you've ever done? Don't have regrets. Don't miss opportunities. Otherwise, you may never know how many people you could have helped.

Here are some insights on **Leadership Vaues** that you can continue to reflect upon.

◆ How is your faith showing up at work? Are you authentically trusting in someone greater than yourself to work in situations that you can't control?

◆ What might your employees be afraid of, even if seems like displaced fear to you? How might that be impacting their progress?

◆ How disciplined is your behavior as you set an example for all of your employees to follow?

◆ How strong is your team? Do you stick together no matter what, and do you have a clear strategy to win?

◆ Are you communicating in a way that helps everyone understand the why of your business priorities? Are you engaging them in strategies for change?

◆ Do you make decisions based on what you believe others expect of you, or based on your own values and priorities?

◆ Are you willing to stand alone and take a different position or approach to an issue when you strongly believe it's the right thing to do? Or will you fold to the pressure of herd mentality?

◆ How are you investing in your own growth and development?

Stay committed to your values. Share the best of who you are. And keep growing.

Step 4.

Distinguishing characteristics of successful leaders

The next set of articles is on **Leadership Traits**—the personality characteristics of successful leaders. Many traits are rooted in increasing emotional intelligence, including self-awareness of how you are perceived and social awareness to manage relationships with others. This vantage point gives you the ability to build engaging connections with colleagues to accomplish organizational goals. As leaders progress to more senior positions, research shows that emotional intelligence is a much greater key to their success. Think about how your emotions play a critical role in each of the following articles.

1. PRIORITIZING RELATIONSHIPS
Good Leaders Follow the Right Instinct

"Good instincts tell you what to do long before your head has figured it out."

—MICHAEL BURKE, RETIRED AMERICAN SOCCER PLAYER

Kelley is stressed. He and his team are on a tight deadline to bring a project to market. If successful, it could significantly boost his company's revenues for the fiscal year. The handoff from the development team to Kelley's team was delayed due to technical issues, and the whole project got backed up. The pressure is intense. The executive committee is now asking for weekly progress reports to ensure their promises to prospective clients and the shareholders will be met.

At the same time, Kelley is exasperated with his team for several errors they've made, along with their pushback on part of the strategy that was previously agreed upon. This morning it reached the point where he blew up and let them have it. His words in the brief team meeting were partly uncontrolled anger and partly controlled manipulation. He wanted to make a point and motivate them to stay sharp and move quicker, and have them understand the pressure he is experiencing.

What Kelley neglected to realize, though, was that his behavior drove them further into their perception of feeling disrespected and unappreciated, and it actually widened the emotional gulf between them. They see Kelley as being part of the problem. No one wants to work for him, and they certainly don't feel like putting forth their best effort. Both sides blame each other and are caught in a behavioral loop that is spiraling out of control. The more Kelley pushes, the more they resist.

Now, Kelley isn't completely emotionally unintelligent. As he drove into work pondering what he would say to his team, he contemplated taking a softer approach. He considered communicating that he believed in their ability to complete the project, on time and under budget. He thought about complimenting some of the members for resolving several unexpected and particularly thorny issues. He also recognized they had put in a lot of hours, foregoing family obligations on behalf of the company. But in the middle of that thought, he got a call from the CFO, ranting about the need to get the job done and avoid a financially negative impact.

What Did Kelley Do Wrong?

Kelley created a negative narrative in his mind, where he saw himself as a victim of everyone else's shortcomings. As a victim, he could justify blaming the company officers, other departments, and his own team for the current predicament. He temporarily absolved himself of the responsibility for correcting his own failures in the matter. Unfortunately, any comfort from that was short-lived because the problem persisted. And Kelley is still accountable for the results. Blaming others was the wrong instinct—it left him with no viable relationships, so he couldn't partner with others for the tasks ahead.

What Kelley Should Have Done Instead

Kelley's instinct was to do the right thing, which was to be supportive of his team and recognize their hard work. But he neglected to make a commitment to follow that instinct and nurture them. Here are three ways Kelley could have done so:

■ **Put relationships before tasks.**
Since work can only be accomplished through people, it makes sense to put our relationships with them ahead of the work that needs to be done. Get to know each person individually. Understand their beliefs and values, their strengths and development needs, and let them get to know you. This builds mutual trust and respect, and becomes the "grease" that gets things done quickly later. Remember that a kind word goes a long way.

■ **Understand motivations and preferences.**
Know what motivates your team and what's important to them in life. Some people need to feel their expertise is recognized, others need pleasant words or a thank you. Some need to see the big picture before the details, or vice versa. Some want their ideas to be heard or to participate in developing the strategy. Some operate best in crisis mode. Some are well networked internally or externally and can gather helpful information and resources. Know them, then let them play to their strengths.

■ **Don't try to change others, change yourself.**
When we try to change others, we're operating from the premise that something is wrong with them. When we instead focus on changing what is wrong with our own thinking or behavior, we exhibit greater respect for others and create a shift in the relationship.

The Right Instinct

The right instinct is often present, but sometimes pushed away and muted as being unimportant, based on the challenges we face. When we learn to pause and listen to that voice, we build positive interactions to support meeting our goals. With practice, the priorities noted above become ingrained in our thinking and behavior, and we authentically demonstrate greater care and concern for others. So, follow your right instinct.

2. YOUR PERSONAL BRAND
5 Keys to Maximizing It

*"Your brand is what people say about
you when you're not in the room."*

—JEFF BEZOS, AMAZON FOUNDER, PRESIDENT, AND CEO

D o you know what people are saying about you when you're not in the room? Do you know what they think of your performance, your presence, your purpose, and your personality? Rather than being unconcerned about what others think, it's important to ensure that *their* perception of you aligns with how *you* want to be perceived. The answers to these questions are part of your personal brand.

Glenn Llopis describes personal brand as "the total experience of someone having a relationship with who you are and what you represent as an individual, as a leader."[25] It's your promise that you will do what you said you will do. It's your reputation that attracts others to you or pushes them away. Establishing and managing your brand is an ongoing process fueled by continual behavioral inputs that remind others of who you are, what you do, and how you can support them. Leaders must develop their brand so that it validates their work, provides a platform to connect with others, and accomplishes their goals.

Managing your personal brand shouldn't be confused with self-promotion. It isn't calling attention to yourself simply for personal gain. Instead, it is clarifying your expertise and value to others to maximize your ability to complement a larger goal or agenda. It's about the team; you are part of a whole.

Brands connect people to things that they value and are a means for identifying people with whom you want to work or build relationships. Developing and managing your brand is an investment in your future.

It's All about Leadership

Leaders have several traits to focus on in developing and managing their personal brands. Each trait is a lever that can be used to communicate and build relationships with others.

- **Leadership Presence**
  Presence is how you "show up" in a room. Like it or not, looks do matter, but it's not about mere physical appearance. It's about conveying the inner confidence and capability to accomplish the challenges in front of you. That means your composure, your demeanor, and your body language should all align. Your attire must connect with your audience, whether it's a hoodie or a suit. You must be aware of the positional and personal power you hold, and be willing to use it appropriately in your role. Your communication style must be clear and compelling to influence those around you.

- **Leadership Purpose**
  Purpose forms the "why" of your leadership. It requires thoughtful introspection to understand the impact you want to make on your environment, and to identify the areas of your work that fuel your passion. It results in focusing less on work that is assigned to you, and instead engaging in work that aligns with your passion. There's a saying that the two most important days in your life are the day you're born and the day you find out why. Leadership

purpose connects you with the specific things you are uniquely gifted and designed to accomplish.

■ **Leadership Strengths**

Strengths include the capabilities and critical success factors necessary to operate in your purpose. Review feedback from performance reviews, mentors, leaders, peers, coaches, and assessments to clarify your strengths. Sometimes others see us quite differently than we see ourselves. Focus your career pursuits on roles that enable you to display these strengths, because that's where you'll be most successful. And while you need to understand your weaknesses, the goal is simply to make sure they don't become a career derailer. Learn from them, but don't try to force yourself into a position that requires you to be very capable in those areas.

■ **Leadership Learning**

Learning sets the stage for you to work effectively in a changing environment. Are you open to learning and receptive to feedback? Can you adapt to a variety of leadership styles based on the situation? Learning can be derived from on-the-job experiences, coaching, training, reading, and openness to diverse perspectives. Learning agility, or the ability and willingness to learn from experience, and subsequently apply that learning to perform successfully under new or first-time conditions, is an important factor.

■ **Leadership Personality**

Your leadership personality is your unique pattern of feeling, thinking, and behaving that defines you. It is a preference that is generally stable throughout your life. And when you understand yourself as a leader, you're better equipped to manage your style to optimize your team's productivity in the context of your environment. Assessments such as DiSC, the Myers–Briggs

Type Inventory, or StrengthsFinder 2.0 can provide a descriptive explanation of your leadership personality and style. Other assessments of emotional intelligence are helpful for feedback on your level of self-awareness, which impacts your relationships.

Think for a moment about someone you know very well. Describe them in the context of their presence, purpose, strengths, learning, and personality. These characteristics are likely the traits that attract you to this person and solidify your relationship. You know what to expect when you interact with them and you depend on them fulfilling their brand promise.

Brands Require Action

So now that you know what a personal brand is, and you know how to grow it, here are the action steps you can take to demonstrate your brand to others:

1. **Market yourself.**

   Build a network of colleagues inside and outside your organization. Don't work with your head down, just focusing on your projects or current environment. Keep your head up, always aware of what's going on internal and external to the organization. Interact with people who are as smart or smarter than you to debate ideas, discuss trends, and generate learning. Use social media to communicate your brand, and make sure you know what comes up when you Google your name.

2. **Learn to dance.**

   With the fast pace of change these days, you must be flexible to quickly adjust to shifting demands in your environment, shifts in meeting discussions, and the rush-pause of projects. Learn to flow with the ups and downs by making sure you have a toolbox of skill sets, and that you know how to pull out what you need from it in any given situation.

3. Be authentic.

Don't pretend to be someone else or adjust your personality just to fit in with the crowd. The disconnect will show up pretty quickly as you fail to establish valuable rapport with your colleagues. It will also be stressful for you. If you don't value the same things as your colleagues, and you don't share similar strengths or interests, maybe you're in the wrong place. Find an environment that complements your personality and supports you in your goals.

4. Establish boundaries.

Know your internal values and guiding principles, and what behaviors are acceptable for you. For example, how you will treat others or respond to their inappropriate behavior, and what value do you place on organizational issues like diversity and inclusion, employee development, customer service, or corporate social responsibility? Communicate these values to others by proactively sharing stories in advance on why those values are important to you. In this way, your colleagues will understand how to best interact with you and when to engage you in initiatives that align with your values. They will also understand behaviors that are not acceptable in your organization and that don't support the culture you're trying to shape.

Finally, your brand must be a good fit, in the right environment or target market. It should connect with others in a way that meets their needs and adds value to them. Just make sure you know what others are saying when you're not in the room.

25. Glenn Llopis, "Personal Branding Is a Leadership Requirement, Not a Self-Promotion Campaign," *Forbes*, April 8, 2013, https://www.forbes.com/sites/glennllopis/2013/04/08/personal-branding-is-a-leadership-requirement-not-a-self-promotion-campaign/#2323e1fe226f.

3. BUILDING TRUSTING RELATIONSHIPS
The Foundation for Growth

"People may hear your words,
but they feel your attitude."

—JOHN MAXWELL, AUTHOR, SPEAKER ON LEADERSHIP

While many of us intellectually understand the importance of building trusting relationships, we don't always demonstrate it. Consider the case of Cathy. She was recently appointed as vice president, responsible for relationship management with her firm's largest client. Interactions between the client and her predecessor became rocky and Cathy must move quickly to smooth things out. Further, she must prove her company can provide value-added products and services. The fact that Cathy's company was voted by an industry panel as providing "best in class" products doesn't carry enough weight. It's all about building a trusting relationship so the customer feels their needs are being met.

And then there's Derek. He just joined a major, fast, casual restaurant chain and is tasked with turning around its relationship with franchisees, which has become contentious over the past several years. The company is trying to convince the franchisees to invest money in upgrading their stores and offering new menu options. But first Derek must restore trust that corporate marketing strategies will drive traffic to the stores and increase revenue. Derek is not fully convinced the company has the right plans, but he needs to quickly understand its needs and make sure there is proper alignment.

Cathy and Derek are preparing for their first meetings with their respective stakeholders. In addition to learning the business challenges, studying market analytics, and reviewing contractual provisions, they both need to promptly build trusting relationships.

Everyone has faced similar situations that play out in their interactions with colleagues and clients on a regular basis. Because trust is the foundation of all human interaction, we must pay particular attention to demonstrating to others that we value them. Here are six steps that facilitate the process for building solid relationships.

1. **Understand trust triggers.**

   Each of us has "touch points" that will trigger an increase or decrease in the level of trust we have for those with whom we're interacting. One trigger could be failing to listen to the details we want to provide on an issue. Other triggers may be their failure to acknowledge our experience level, or not respecting our need to share the context for certain situations. For example, one of my coaching clients has a need to spend 5 to 10 minutes at the beginning of every meeting talking about family and personal activities. He needs to reaffirm our coaching-client relationship and get comfortable. Another coaching client sits down and quickly shares a concern that is bothering her, and we go from there. At our initial meetings, I had to listen to each person as an individual and learn their communication style, then adjust my own style to build that initial trust. If I didn't pay attention to these triggers, it would negatively impact my ability to support their growth.

2. **Learn passion points.**

   We all have an underlying motive for the work that we do; a sense of what drives us and shapes our values. It may be finding new ways to use technology to solve problems, ensuring fair treatment in the workplace, or finding a competitive advantage to whatever product we're marketing. In many cases, our decisions emanate from this passion point. Thus, it's important to spend time getting to know colleagues by understanding why they have chosen their line of work, what's fulfilling about it to them, and what parts of their roles are most rewarding. Once you have a better sense of what drives them, you can target your conversation to these aspects of their work to demonstrate respect and forge an alliance.

3. **Encourage the work of others.**
I'm fortunate to have many colleagues who are doing amazing work in a variety of fields. I admittedly don't have the depth of information to understand all of it, and many of our interactions simply don't require me to do so. But, if I care about them, I've found I can easily take a moment to encourage them. Sometimes this involves 15 minutes to help them analyze an interpersonal situation and find a way to better handle it. Other times, it's a listening ear to empathize with their challenges and urge them to stick with it. Either way, they know that I care.

4. **Observe good body language.**
How do you feel when you sit down to talk with a colleague and they keep watching their phone, fiddling with an object, or looking over your shoulder to see who else is in the room? These behaviors tend to cut the conversation short, minimize the level of sharing, and weaken the relationship. In fact, 10 minutes of focused attention is better than 30 minutes of distracted time. We all know our body language is important in building relationships, however, we too frequently fail to manage it. Good eye contact, leaning in, full body alignment, and clarifying the amount of time for the conversation are critical components of making sure the other person feels the interaction is valuable to you.

5. **Repeat what you heard.**

   Good listeners pay attention to what is being said and can repeat it. This reaffirms you heard the person and provides an opportunity for mutual clarification and understanding. It also gives you time to think about what was said so you can respond thoughtfully. You may immediately have an answer to the person's issue, but if it were that easy, they would have thought of it themselves. Often, there is a deeper challenge that needs to be discussed and teased out. They want to be heard, they want to be respected, they want to find their own solution, and you can aid them along the way.

6. **Do what you say, say what you'll do.**

   Be authentic. Deliver on your promises. Avoid vague statements. Clarify the things you can and can't control. Keep confidences. Ensure your behavior aligns with the fact that you truly care about their concerns.

   Continuous attention to these six steps will enable Cathy and Derek to establish a foundation of trust and confidence with their stakeholders. Then they can build upon that trust to address their business challenges.

4. EMPATHETIC LEADERSHIP
Becoming a Leader Who Cares

"Empathy is patiently and sincerely seeing the world through the other person's eyes. It's not learned in school. It's cultivated over a lifetime."

—ALBERT EINSTEIN, GERMAN MATHEMATICIAN, PHYSICIST, AND NOBEL PRIZE WINNER WHO DEVELOPED THE THEORY OF RELATIVITY

I recently had an opportunity to interact with a variety of people in a service-based organization for a prolonged period of time. The nature of these interactions was often stressful for myself and those around me. Performance of their job duties required a high level of quality control and process focus. To break the tension, I occasionally joked with them that they needed to avoid making any errors because it would require them to complete too much paperwork.

But after a while, I began to realize that despite the pressure of their roles, most of them displayed a remarkable level of empathy. They didn't simply *act* like they cared about their client population, they really *did* seem to understand, and they actively advocated for them. It struck me that many of these individuals are not only in roles that are appropriately aligned with their giftedness, but they are part of an organization that genuinely cares about their work. This led me to think about the culture and "feel" in many other organizations, and to wonder how employees, clients, and other stakeholders experience them in the context of empathy.

Understanding Empathy

Empathy is the capacity to understand or feel what another person is experiencing from within the other person's frame of reference (Wikipedia). As one of the core areas of emotional intelligence, it demonstrates an awareness of others, in terms of what they're feeling and how those feelings arise. It is placing yourself in another person's shoes and activating not just your physical senses, but your intellectual and emotional senses to identify with their feelings. Conversely, leaders who lack empathy make decisions without considering the desires and reactions of people, and the impact of those decisions. They may also fail to communicate effectively.

Organizations that place a high value on empathy recognize that engaged and connected employees and clients are part of the key to their success. They understand the importance of delivering results and accomplishing objectives, and they know that how you do it is as important as getting it done. Their leaders set the example through their behavior and the leadership priorities they use in decision-making.

Empathetic Leaders CARE

Leaders who care about their teams are purposeful in demonstrating behaviors that communicate empathy. Here are four common traits they display:

1. **Compassion**

   They demonstrate tangible concern when others go through adversity. Rather than constantly putting on the "corporate face" or approaching every issue based on business needs, they focus on addressing the human needs. For example, companies whose employees are impacted by tornadoes or earthquakes will adjust company policies to support them and their families until they get back on their feet.

2. **Approachability**

When employees know their leaders care about them, they feel comfortable interacting with them in formal and informal settings. Such leaders typically make it a point to reach out to employees and talk with them about a variety of business and nonbusiness events. You may find such leaders sharing lunch with a table of employees in the cafeteria, initiating conversation with team members in the hallway, or remembering personal aspects of peoples' lives.

3. **Relatability**

These leaders are transparent in sharing experiences that demonstrate what they have in common with others in the organization. They emphasize common needs and challenges, along with ensuring equal treatment at all levels. These leaders pepper their commentary with information that shows their humanness and the ups and downs of life. Sheryl Sandberg, COO of Facebook, has dealt rather publicly with the sudden death in May 2015 of her husband, David Goldberg. She demonstrates that such experiences impact everyone, regardless of socioeconomic or organizational level, and we all "bring them to work" to deal with in some capacity.

4. **Encouragement**

These leaders are genuinely interested in the best outcomes for others. They will support employees' personal and professional goals, even if it appears they may need to leave the company to attain them. One company in western Michigan has its employees meet with managers to establish personal, professional, and financial goals. Their focus on employees has reduced annual turnover to less than 10 percent, and increased customer retention to 98 percent. Their motto is "Take good care of your people and they'll take good care of your clients."

CAREing Leaders Take Action

Effective empathy is best coupled with corresponding action. As a leader, once you understand this level of social awareness, it is incumbent upon you to make leadership decisions that reflect this value.

Years ago, I was a part of an organization that went through a significant downsizing initiative. It was very painful and very public. Overall, we attempted to communicate frequently with employees to let them know what was happening and why. We tried to anticipate their concerns and respond to them, and encouraged leaders to have candid conversations with their teams. Employees at all levels were impacted, and even those who remained had a range of emotions. At a team level, those leaders who demonstrated greater empathy with their employees rebounded faster and became productive more quickly.

Recently, a colleague told me about a newly appointed CEO who conducted an employee town hall meeting his first day on the job. He noted to those gathered that their employee engagement scores had increased in the past year and asked them why. They responded that under his predecessor's leadership, they finally felt they had a leader who cared about them. Not surprisingly, given his priority on meeting with employees, the new CEO had a similar value and was committed to continuing that approach.

These examples support the familiar phrase "Employees don't care how much you know until they know how much you care." And they'll never know how much you care until you show them.

5. THE REWARD OF WAITING
Should Leaders Really Be Patient?

*"The two most powerful warriors
are patience and time."*

—LEO TOLSTOY, RUSSIAN WRITER

L eaders are typically rewarded for taking action. They're used to being in control and working to influence the environment around them. They have a vision, mission, and objectives to accomplish. Other stakeholders hold them accountable for developing and executing plans to drive results. Providing excuses isn't part of their vocabulary. So what place does the word "patience" have in the context of leadership?

For a better understanding, let's look at patience as a leadership competency. According to Michael Lombardo and Robert Eichinger's model of leadership, here are some differences exhibited by patient leaders and those who are not so patient.

Patient Leaders
- Are tolerant with people and processes
- Wait for others to catch up before acting
- Try to understand people and data before making decisions and proceeding
- Follow established processes

143

Leaders Unskilled in Patience

- Act before it's time to act
- Don't take the time to listen or understand
- Think almost everything needs to be done shorter and quicker
- Often interrupt others and finish their sentences
- Are action oriented and avoid process and problem complexity
- Sometimes jump to conclusions instead of thinking things through [26]

Now I'm sure you can think of a number of leaders who have demonstrated a lack of patience. How did you feel about working with them? Were you exasperated? Did you do your best to avoid them? Did you devise strategies to work around them or try to get them to understand a particular point of view? Yet their impatience prevented them from getting the best work from you and others on their team, and maximizing results.

Learning to be patient means learning to wait, pause, listen, and think. It requires acceptance of the fact that you can't control or influence the outcome you desire in every situation. It does not however, mean doing nothing. It involves an active state of mind and focusing on the desired result, along with taking action within one's sphere of control.

Proper Patience

When is exercising patience the appropriate thing to do? Here are some examples.

1. **Right position/right person**

    In my work, I interact with a number of leaders who are seeking new positions and organizations who are seeking new leaders. Position seekers polish their résumés to reflect their strongest skills, actively network, and put their best foot forward in interviews. Organizations write robust position descriptions, identify the best search strategy, and conduct detailed interviews. But neither can fully control finding the right match of person to position. Position seekers lament not getting the job they really wanted, and organizations lament not being able to snare that elusive "purple squirrel." There's a fit that comes naturally when the right person meets the right position, and you can't force it. Unfortunately, I have many examples of impatient position seekers who acted too quickly and accepted the wrong offer, and organizations that, in their haste, failed to thoroughly evaluate a candidate.

2. **Listening to others' points of view**
Patient leaders exhibit respect for the people they work with because they recognize three basic tenants. First, they know they can't think of everything themselves and they *need* to surround themselves with smart people who will contribute to the organization's results. Second, they understand the need to thoughtfully evaluate situations and identify appropriate options. And third, they recognize that diversity of thought always yields better results.

3. **Process focus**
Patient leaders recognize the importance of clearly understood and communicated processes and procedures. Impatient leaders want to skip steps in the name of driving faster results and getting to the end. Instead, it's critical to have experts design processes where each step is well thought out, necessary, and streamlined, and to ensure all stakeholders understand the value it provides.

4. **Economy and environment**
This is the big one. No matter how hard you try, there are variables that are completely outside of your control and influence. Look at recent economic downturns. While many leaders will go to great lengths to influence these situations, you can't make people buy your product or service. You can't make people spend their money. You can't fully control consumer sentiment. You can't make mergers and acquisitions happen. You can't fully predict the future. You have to optimize the variables that you can control, then be patient as you wait for things to change, and try to understand and anticipate how they'll change.

Your Test of Patience

Every leader faces the challenge of demonstrating patience in both simple and complex situations. A leader's ability to respond appropriately is a demonstration of maturity. It involves a mental perspective of peace in the midst of uncertainty and avoiding self-damaging behavior while anticipating future outcomes.

Oscar Munoz likely faced the greatest test of patience in his life when he suffered a heart attack in October 2015, 38 days after taking over as CEO of United Airlines.[27] Almost three months later, he had a heart transplant and returned to work several months thereafter. Obsessed with fitness and a committed vegan, Munoz probably never expected his heart to fail. He assumed leadership of United Airlines when it was still trying to recover from a disastrous merger several years earlier with Continental Airlines, and was in the midst of strife with multiple unions. His career to date had been filled with successful roles at multiple companies. He was used to being in control and turning ailing businesses around. But there's nothing a transplant candidate can do to make a donor heart available. It requires a new level of patience and maintaining a positive mindset during the wait.

Your challenge is to prepare now to better handle your own tests of patience. Big or small, complex or simple, these situations will find you, and you get to choose how you will respond.

26. Michael M. Lombardo and Robert W. Eichinger, FYI: *For Your Improvement—A Development and Coaching Guide*, (Minneapolis: Lominger Limited, Inc., 1996).

27. Shawn Tully, "How United's Oscar Munoz Bounced Back after a Heart Attack," *Fortune*, November 18, 2016, https://fortune.com/longform/united-airlines-ceo-oscar-munoz/.

6. WHEN LEADING YOU IS ALL ABOUT ME
The Self-Absorbed Leader

*"A strong and secure leader accepts blame
and gives credit. A weak and insecure
leader gives blame and takes credit."*

—COACH JOHN WOODEN, LEGENDARY HEAD COACH FOR THE
UNIVERSITY OF CALIFORNIA, LOS ANGELES, FROM 1948 TO 1975

T rue leadership is about influencing others to achieve common goals. But when leaders place too great a focus on their own self-concept, status, and personal goals, this self-absorption is generally driven by feelings of *insecurity* or *superiority*. These feelings drive behaviors at opposite ends of the spectrum and stifle the growth and development of the team and organization. Let's look at examples.

Insecure Leadership
Chris is the CEO of a multinational company. As he banged his fist on the conference room table, his frustration was palpable to those in the room. Joe, the vp of product development, has worked for Chris for a year. He joined the firm enticed by the scope of responsibility in this vp position, and by Chris's excitement and commitment to developing

a new product line. However, now Joe is wondering how much longer he can endure working there. Having moved his family halfway across the country, Joe wants to give it his best effort, but his natural optimism has waned sharply.

Every week in Chris's staff meeting, Joe and his colleagues review the same issues with seemingly no progress. Chris asks detailed questions on obscure topics, is obsessed with short-term metrics, and is intolerant of any appearance of a mistake, misunderstanding, or missed goal. Chris frequently yells or curses at his direct reports when they are unable to answer his questions, or for their apparent failings. He rarely leaves his office to meet with employees or customers, and he lacks a sense of reality about challenges the business is facing.

Joe and his teammates have learned to take additional time before these meetings to "get their story straight," or "rearrange" data to make it look good, just to avoid the verbal harangue. They never know who is going to be in the hot seat next. Meanwhile, they all know that in spite of the favorable quarterly reports, the business isn't meeting customer needs, nor keeping pace with innovation in the market. It's just a matter of time before the shareholders turn on them. Yet there is no way anyone will confront Chris with the negative impact of his leadership style.

Superior Leadership

Across town at another major company, Pat, the CEO, is having a great day. She just returned from a trip visiting several plants and was pumped up by the reception she received. The "troops" were all gathered to meet her helicopter as it landed. Her announcement of bringing new work to the plants was met with the expected cheers, and the union leadership was exuberant. Pat met with community leaders and the media recap was fantastic.

It irritated Pat a bit that the plant managers were more reserved. They each had tried to insert too much time for one-on-one discussions about issues at their respective plants. One seemed concerned about allocation of funds to upgrade the machinery to ensure they could meet new production goals. The other was nervous about recent tests of water quality at the plant, possibly a result of the manufacturing processes. Pat made sure the plant managers understood they are responsible for managing these issues successfully at the local level or they'll lose their jobs.

Pat doesn't have time for those details, nor for other "bright ideas" on growing the business from her leadership team. She is focused on strategies to maximize the company's market capitalization. And she is in talks to buy out a major competitor that could result in having a lock on the market. If all goes well, she could end up heading the largest company of its type and greatly expand her compensation package. So she wants to make sure nothing interrupts the success of this deal.

The Same Impact

Chris's insecurities as a leader are evident to all. His obsession over details and tongue lashings after any small misstep mute his team's willingness to investigate new ideas. Pat's attitude of superiority is stifling, and her team is aware that every event should be an opportunity to reinforce her status. As leaders, their styles may be very different, yet they are similar because they're both mired in self-absorption. Their decisions are driven by how they will be perceived. And their leadership isn't characterized by focusing on their teams, organizational goals, meeting stakeholder needs, or adding value to others. Instead, their motto is "It's all about me," and they may well believe that their leadership adds priceless value to their respective companies.

We all would like to hope Chris and Pat exemplify extreme versions of this self-absorbed behavior. But I'll confess that I've had at least a moment (some might say two or three) when I felt insecure as a leader, and it negatively impacted my leadership results. Similarly, there were a few times when I was caught up in the midst of my critical role in addressing a major business crisis, only to be brought back to earth by a call from my mother that required patient listening. I'm thankful for both of these learning opportunities.

The Shift

Self-absorbed leaders will only mature and shift their behavior when they begin to value others as greater than themselves. They need to recognize the key to their organization's success lies in bringing out the best in their people. Gaining this level of security requires a balance of humility and self-confidence.

Think about the following behaviors and where you might be displaying traits of self-absorption. Recognition of how your behavior impacts others is the first step in making this shift.

Self-absorbed Leaders	Self-confident Leaders
Dominate the conversation with stories of their greatness	Pull great stories out of others
Demand loyalty from others	Demonstrate loyalty to others
Inhibit critical conversations	Lean into understanding the underlying drivers blocking business results
Have all the great ideas themselves	Surround themselves with others who have great ideas
Tear others down	Build others up
Can't handle the truth	Speak the truth
Are resistant to change	Are open to growth and development
Create negative talk about others to justify their own behavior	Create positive talk about others to reinforce others' good behaviors

What behaviors are you engaging in to demonstrate greater self-confidence in your leadership?

7. LEADERSHIP STAMINA
The Priority of Self-Management

"To maintain success, stamina is more important than talent. You have to learn to be a marathon runner."

—JOAN RIVERS, COMEDIAN, ACTRESS, WRITER,
PRODUCER, AND TELEVISION HOST

How often do you find yourself working long hours on a major organizational project, leading your team, managing diverse stakeholder opinions, or facing a looming deadline with not enough resources (time, people, money, technology) to meet your goals? Then somehow, it all comes together, and you're a hero! A superhero! Or so you think. In reality, you realize you've thrown all your energy into this one facet of your life and work, and other facets (family, relationships, other projects, personal finances, exercise, life goals, etc.) are now suffering from lack of attention.

About 20 years ago, when I was completing my doctoral dissertation, I simultaneously received a coveted promotion to a new and very demanding role at work. I knew it would be difficult, but I thought I could somehow get it all done. Well, I was right and wrong. I managed those two priorities, however, my relationships and emotions suffered. I thought I had an "S" for superhero on my chest, yet in reality, that "S"

151

was torn and tattered, and held in place by crazy glue, safety pins, and duct tape!

Leaders become superheroes at the expense of other priorities in their lives. But superheroes are fiction, with strength and abilities beyond the capabilities of the normal human being. And we're all normal human beings. So instead of trying to be superheroes, we should learn *leadership stamina*.

Stamina as a Priority

Leadership stamina involves managing your mental, emotional, and physical strength to operate in an intense environment and move past roadblocks to accomplish objectives. Real leadership means influencing others to accomplish a significant goal. And if you're aiming high enough, those goals are never easy. You'll be challenged to give up, downsize, settle, or compromise along the way. You'll have to balance other priorities competing for your time and energy. But most of all, you'll need to care for yourself to ensure that gain in one area doesn't come at the expense of loss in another.

Professional athletes know how to make *leadership stamina* a priority. They typically engage in rituals to focus every aspect of their mind, body, and interactions with others to maximize their performance. Similarly, business leaders must balance their constant meeting schedules and deadlines, along with other demands on their time, to ensure consistent high performance.

I recently completed a meeting with a client that involved facilitating a three-day training. I knew this would be an intense time, requiring focus on each individual in the room to ensure the learning experience was impactful. As a result, I planned in advance what I needed to do to manage my stamina during that process. It included getting necessary rest, eating nutritious foods, exercising, and avoiding mental distractions from a volume of email.

6 Tips for Self-Management

So, how do you build and manage your *leadership stamina*? Here are several tips.

1. **Emotional energy**

   Know how you recharge emotionally. For some (us introverts), it's through quiet times of reflection and rest. For others (you extraverts), it's through having fun and spending time with friends. Set boundaries to avoid permitting people or things to drain your energy or invade your private space. Ensure you have a peaceful spot in which to retreat, or an activity to divert your attention when necessary.

2. **Physical energy**

   Pay attention to your body's sleep patterns to ensure you get sufficient rest. You may be able to go for a short period of time with minimal sleep, but there will be a day of reckoning when you'll have to catch up. Recognize the symptoms of exhaustion—it may manifest as sickness, irritability, or poor decisions. Over-reaching physically can result in illness that will leave you even further behind.

3. **Nutrition**

   I'm amazed at the number of leaders who tell me they regularly skip or don't eat balanced meals, either because they're too busy or don't think it's necessary. And still others are battling chronic diseases. Just like your vehicle won't run well on cheap gas, your body needs optimal fuel to perform. Consult an expert to figure out what you need to do to become and remain healthy, and make it a priority in your life. If you become sick, your colleagues may miss you, but they can and will survive without you. Don't force their hand.

4. **Mental acuity**

   Know what time of day your energy level and creative abilities are highest and schedule the appropriate work during that timeframe. Some people like to get up at 4 a.m. and work, others prefer to burn the midnight oil, while still others know to schedule their most serious meetings in the middle of the day. Identify distracting thoughts, people, and environments to ensure you optimize the right setting for your work, as well at the type of work (collaborative, thought generating, emails, writing, etc.) to accomplish.

5. **Presence**

   Be aware of how you leverage your body movements and physical appearance to connect and communicate with others. Your body language can convey confidence and attract and motivate others to engage with you.

6. **Motivation**

   This is the basis for all stamina—when you're motivated by your inner purpose to accomplish a goal. Motivation underpins the ability to persevere in the midst of circumstances that would normally cause you to give up. It's based on your underlying values of what is important in life, and your mission for and vision of the future.

Finally, *leadership stamina* requires discipline to balance all of these variables in any given environment. Be aware of your unique characteristics and integrate all facets of your life at the level that is ideal for you. Your capacity isn't infinite. Prioritize your self-management. Know when to ask for help, hire help, take a break, and protect yourself. Establish sacred times and spaces to recharge and get your creative juices flowing. People may pull you in a number of directions, so you must set your boundaries up front regarding what you need in order to optimize your performance.

LEADERSHIP TRAIT REFLECTIONS

Has your self-awareness become heightened on your leadership learning journey? Did you have flashbacks as you read about these leadership traits? Sometimes they remind us of situations where we displayed the "right" behaviors, and other times we're reminded of situations where we wished we had behaved differently. The good news is we all have opportunities for continued improvement.

Here are some questions on **Leadership Traits** that you may find helpful:

◆ Where are you placing results before relationships?
◆ What's your brand and is it serving you well?
◆ Where do you need to quickly build trusting relationships with your stakeholders?
◆ Where do you need to practice more empathy with your colleagues?
◆ Where is your patience being tested and how are you responding?
◆ Where are you feeling insecure or superior in your leadership roles, and how can you make the necessary adjustment?
◆ How are you practicing healthy habits to ensure you have the stamina to accomplish your goals?

Growth in each of these areas includes learning emotionally intelligent practices that positively impact relationships and results.

Step 5.

LEADERSHIP
BEHAVIORS

Actions and attitudes that support constructive leadership

T he next set of articles is about **Leadership Behaviors.** They are the actions and attitudes that support constructive leadership and are the outward manifestation of our values. It's what we *do* on a daily basis. Typically, companies post their values on the walls of their lobbies, conference rooms, and hallways. Then you observe the behaviors of the people who work there and find out what they *really* believe. The employees pay more attention to their leaders' behaviors than to the words on the walls; they know what behaviors are rewarded. This vantage point is the practical application of how leaders navigate through tough business challenges, particularly given constant pressure to perform well.

Think of leaders you've worked closely with, whose values and behaviors are aligned. Now think of several others who say one thing but do another, and how their teams respond to this disconnect. You have an opportunity to make a difference in this area.

1. SERVANT LEADERSHIP
Heart, Head, and Hands

"The servant-leader is servant first. It begins with the natural feeling that one wants to serve, to serve first. Then conscious choice brings one to aspire to lead."

—ROBERT K. GREENLEAF, FOUNDER OF GREENLEAF
CENTER FOR SERVANT LEADERSHIP

Several centuries ago, during the Revolutionary War, a group of soldiers were trying to move a heavy piece of lumber that was blocking the road. As hard as they tried, over and over, they couldn't seem to move it across the ground. Their corporal stood nearby giving them direction, and probably graciously allowed them a brief period of rest. He may have even sought their input on "how" to best move the huge piece of wood. But after their repeated, unsuccessful attempts, his patience was wearing thin.

159

Another more senior army officer came along on horseback and observed the men's efforts. After a moment, he suggested the corporal help his men. With a tinge of offense in his voice, the corporal responded, "Me? Why, I'm a corporal, sir!"

The senior officer dismounted his horse and stepped over to the men. He positioned himself alongside them and gave the order to "heave." All of a sudden the timber moved into the position where they needed it, no longer blocking the pathway.

The officer then turned to the corporal and told him, "The next time you have a piece of timber for your men to move, just call the commander-in-chief." The officer was George Washington, then commander-in-chief of the Continental Army during the Revolutionary War, and later the first U.S. president.

Washington's behavior modeled servant leadership. He led by example; he didn't merely direct others or solicit their input. He demonstrated his willingness to serve and support them. As a result, the soldiers felt his tangible encouragement of their work, and he understood the challenges of their roles.

Leadership in Service

Servant leadership requires engaging the heart, head, and hands of the leader. It means operating with a high degree of self awareness of your values and behaviors that focus on *giving* to others instead of *getting* from them.

Your HEART – Care about and connect with others.

As a leader, you can't effectively connect with your team unless they know you care about them. The corporal's ego wouldn't let him behave in a way that showed care and concern. He felt he was above his men and wasn't interested in building emotional interaction. But Washington immediately demonstrated a willingness to connect with the men and share their burden. They bonded at a heart level.

Your HEAD – Think about what your team needs to perform at their best.

Make it a priority to recognize and develop those skill sets and interests where individual members of your team perform well, and encourage their growth. Utilize leadership and personality assessments to identify their strengths and areas for further development. Be intentional about team building, encouraging collaboration, and strategically positioning members for team and organizational success. Washington quickly assessed where the leverage was most needed and how they should move the log.

Your HANDS – Take action and do something.

Sometimes it's appropriate to guide the team from a distance. At other times, you need to get in the trenches and work shoulder to shoulder with them. The corporal was remiss in understanding the difference. Washington recognized the need immediately. He saw the discouragement in their eyes and knew the importance of the task and speed with which it needed to be accomplished. This was an "all hands on deck" situation. No one was above pitching in and helping.

Two Key Questions

If you want to operate as a servant leader, there are two simple questions you should ask yourself daily:

1. **WHO can I serve?**

   You interact daily with family, employees, clients, suppliers, investors, and other stakeholders. Each one presents an opportunity for service. Do you approach them in terms of how *they can help you* achieve your goal, or do you think about how *you can serve them* and help meet their needs? Focusing on others through the lens of your heart, head, and hands will naturally lead to opportunities to support them.

2. HOW can I serve?

You can take a number of approaches to serve the people around you. But first begin with thinking of others' interests and needs before your own. Your team can't deliver *effectively* on objectives when their needs aren't being met, when they don't feel heard, when they don't feel comfortable discussing concerns or requesting necessary resources.

- First and most importantly, communicate a sense of **purpose**, or the "why" of the work to be performed. Help your team connect their roles and responsibilities to the bigger picture of the value it creates for others.

- Establish an **environment** where high performance is expected, risks are managed, and unnecessary obstacles are removed. Encourage them to fail forward and embrace innovation.

- Position your **product or service** to serve, and focus on your clients, not fulfill your own need for position, power, or personal gain.

- **Empower** your team by identifying and valuing their talents and passions, so you can help them grow into strong servant leaders themselves. Good leaders produce more good leaders.

How Are You Serving?

Servant leadership may manifest differently at various points in your career and life. Consider the following examples:

Pat Curran enjoyed a 25-year career working her way up the corporate ladder at Walmart. She was included in *Fortune* magazine's 50 Most Powerful Women list in 2005. But in 2009, at the young age of 45, she left her career and highly paid role as executive vice president of store operations and went to nursing school. Curran is now working pro bono as a newborn specialist in a hospital in Arkansas. She went back to her original passion of nursing because she wanted the next part of her life to focus on serving and giving.[28] And her phenomenal career success provided the financial security for her to be able to do so.

Scott Harrison spent a decade as a successful nightclub promoter. He indulged in all the excesses that accompanied that role until he realized he was morally, spiritually, and emotionally bankrupt. He sold all of his possessions and spent the next two years volunteering on a hospital ship off the coast of Liberia. During that time, he learned about the lack of clean water available to the people there. When returned to New York, he started Charity: Water, a nonprofit raising money to provide clean, safe drinking water to people in developing countries.

I spent the first 30 years of my career in corporate America, climbing what I perceived to be the "ladder of success." While I learned a tremendous amount about organizational behavior during that time frame, I've since realized that instead of my corporate career being an end in itself, it was the foundation for my current role as an executive coach, consultant, and speaker. Although I had to learn aspects of business development, or getting prospective clients to purchase my services, I've discovered it's so much more relaxing and rewarding to simply talk with prospects from the perspective of understanding how I can best serve *them*. And when I serve them, business opportunities easily present themselves to me.

According to best-selling author and speaker Patrick Lencioni, there's no other type of leadership than servant leadership; all leaders should be servants. How are you bringing servant leadership to your role?

28. Jennifer Reingold, "Why Top Women Are Disappearing From Corporate America," *Fortune*, September 9, 2016, https://fortune.com/longform/women-corporate-america/.

2. MOTIVATIONS TO GOOD DECISIONS
Getting to the Root of the Issue

"Human behavior flows from three main sources: desire, emotion, and knowledge."

—PLATO, GREEK PHILOSOPHER

P am arrived at the office early. She hadn't slept well last night because she was wrestling with an important decision to be made in her executive committee meeting this morning. The committee had been evaluating the development and launch of a new product for the past six months. And today they would make a final decision on whether they were going to move forward. The discussions had been thorough yet difficult, with wide-ranging opinions on what they should do. There is substantial risk associated with the launch, but the potential reward could significantly increase market share. As CEO, Pam needs everyone to make a full commitment to the decision. While the objective, technical analysis is favorable, a number of other issues have arisen, and there has been a LOT of debate.

Jim, vp of sales, is elated with his team's performance over the past year. The current product generated large bonuses for them. A shift to the new replacement product in the coming year would negatively impact those bonuses and morale would surely suffer. Thus, Jim anticipates difficulty retaining his best salespeople, and he isn't sure how to effectively motivate the group.

Maurice, manufacturing vp, is beginning to experience challenges with the equipment used to manufacture the current product. The investment to shift to a new product could provide the necessary funding to support badly needed upgrades in the plants. But his direct report developed the new manufacturing technology and Maurice's own lack of knowledge is glaringly obvious. Thus, Maurice is afraid of the potential threat to his position.

Jenna, the CFO, looks forward to the expected boost in revenue this new product would provide. She purposefully developed a three-year projection showing that the company's profitability would significantly increase and is hopeful the board will consider her a strong successor to the CEO in their upcoming meeting. It is well known among the team that Jenna has lofty career goals.

Jonathan, engineering vp, is not a fan of the new product. He has a different priority for the company strategy and this would take resources away from his pet project. If Jonathan could instead persuade the team to bring the product to market that he has been working on for the past decade, it would elevate his standing among his peers in the industry and potentially lead to a cushy retirement job leading the national professional association.

Objective + Subjective = Good Decisions

Pam's quandary isn't about the quality of analysis leading up to this decision. It's about the motivation driving each leader. Good decisions are the product of a variety of objective factors, as well as subjective factors. They are the *How* and the *Why* of decision-making.

The well-known Myers-Briggs Type Indicator personality assessment provides an effective guide on *How* to make decisions factoring in diverse styles. Called the "Z" Model, it outlines a deliberate sequence of steps that engages all individual preferences involved in the decision process. They are basically as follows:

1. **Address the way a person gathers information.**
   - Ask *Sensing* questions to define the problem, based on the information you take in through your five senses.
   - Ask *Intuitive* questions to consider the possibilities of a sixth sense.

2. **Address the way a person makes decisions.**
   - Ask *Thinking* questions, based on logic, organization, and structure to weigh the consequences of each course of action.
   - Ask *Feeling* questions to weigh the alternatives, based on personal values.

But a powerful driver for decision-making is to understand the *Why*, or the motivation behind the decision. Understanding *Why* can have a greater impact on the quality of decisions than simply understanding *How* to make quality decisions.

Underlying Motivations

Decisions may be motivated by several factors.

- **Abundance versus scarcity**
  Leaders who believe in abundance make decisions based on a belief that there are sufficient resources to invest in people. They give to others and support their growth. Leaders who believe in scarcity make decisions to benefit themselves, frequently at the expense of others. They are not sensitive to those who are forced to do without.

- **Personal conviction versus public praise**
  Leaders who prioritize their personal convictions make decisions based on their core values. Identifying these core values is important in determining cultural fit within organizations. Leaders who desire public praise make decisions that will bring

them recognition and notoriety. They have more of a "me first" approach, ensuring their personal advantage in situations.

- **Purpose versus pressure**
  Leaders who know their unique purpose in life make decisions that will help them accomplish it. They have a deep understanding of their personal *Why* based on their values and personal introspection. Leaders who make decisions responding to pressure focus on what others desire them to do. They shift with the wind and organizational politics.

- **Conscious understanding versus unconscious bias**
  Leaders who make decisions based on conscious understanding take the time to gain a deeper insight into driving factors and they value diversity of thought. Leaders who make decisions based on unconscious bias may negatively and unfairly impact others based on personal prejudices and limited facts.

Bringing It All Together

Pam slipped into her seat a few minutes before starting her executive committee meeting. The time she took after arriving at work to review decision-making processes and motivations gave her a greater sense of direction in how to approach this decision. Pam could see some of the underlying rationales driving each person. Rather than continue the debate of the previous meetings, she framed the decision to be made and walked the group through responding to the questions at each step of the "Z" model. The questions were uncomfortable for everyone as they clung to their closely held positions. But Pat didn't give them a pass. She pressed them to consider all the options and issues and probed their motivations. It was a long meeting, and excruciatingly painful at times. But about two-thirds of the way through, they began to understand the value of the *quality* of discussion they were having. And in the end, everyone understood and bought into the final decision. Pam's attention to not only the *Why* but the *How* of their decision resulted in greater commitment to a successful product launch.

3. WHAT TO DO WHEN YOU DON'T KNOW WHAT TO DO
Waiting for an Answer

"Unsuccessful people make decisions based on their current circumstances, while successful people make decisions based on where they desire to be."

—BENJAMIN HARDY, PH.D., PSYCHOLOGIST, AND AUTHOR

As a leader, the "buck" for certain decisions stops with you. You're responsible for outcomes impacting your team, organization, career, family, and friends. Sometimes the choice is clear, but frequently it's not. Ambiguities are the norm. And while there is pressure to make *fast* decisions, you know it's more important to make *timely* decisions. Meanwhile, stakeholders press you because they have their own agendas and need to know how your decision involves them.

Good decision-making isn't based on the *quantity* of information you're able to review, but on the *quality* of information you're able to comprehend and process to the most appropriate conclusion. Good decision-making brings together intuition and an understanding of the many networks affected by the choices you make. It incorporates *intellectual agility* to draw conclusions from a broad array of facts and data to reach desired outcomes, with the *political savvy* to navigate varied perspectives and power dynamics. Thus, decision-making is not only a science but an art.

So how do you proceed when faced with complex decisions whose solutions are ambiguous and potentially costly? When deadlines are looming, timelines are pressing, interested parties are asking, and budgets are withholding? You've already eliminated several options and narrowed the scope. An obvious choice may be emerging, but you don't yet feel comfortable with it. Something is missing, but you're not sure what it is. What do you do when you don't know what to do?

Wait For It

Across the decades of my career, one of my best learnings was knowing when *not* to make a decision...yet. I learned to listen to my gut, trust my instincts, gather more information, put people off, and sometimes just wait. Invariably, with the passage of a day, a week, or a month, other variables would shift, and more information or perspectives would come into focus that would make the appropriate solution obvious. Had I caved in to earlier pressure to decide, my choice would not have been the best one. This is obviously easier when others trust you and you're perceived as capable in your role, because you invariably must help them understand why you've made or delayed a decision. But even in the absence of trust, a poor-quality decision can do more damage than waiting for the right moment to make that decision.

I'm also reminded of the 1997 movie *Air Force One*, in which Harrison Ford portrays the president of the United States. He, his family, and several members of his cabinet are traveling back to the U.S. aboard his plane when Russian terrorists, on board and disguised as journalists, hijack the plane and are intent on securing the release of a Kazakhstan terrorist leader held by the U.S. military. To save the lives of those held hostage on the plane, the president gives the order to free the terrorist while the U.S. military works to rescue the president. Back in Washington, the defense secretary urges the vice president, played by Glenn Close, to invoke the 25th amendment and remove the president from office so that his order to free the terrorist will not stand. In spite of the incredible pressure to do so, the vice president refuses to sign the executive order, and the president is ultimately rescued before the terrorist leader is fully released. It's obvious her gut instinct was at work, as she and the occupants of the situation room heave a great sigh of relief that her delay paid off.

What Do You Consider?

When you're in that high-pressure situation to make a complex decision, there are three key areas on which to focus that can guide you.

1. **Priorities**—What are your desired *outcomes*?
   Decisions are all about achieving results. Thus, you should clarify what you are trying to accomplish. Sometimes that answer isn't so obvious. Is it more important to increase revenue, sell more products and services, or open more stores? Is it more important to build brand awareness or redesign your product to make it more visibly attractive? Is it more important to retain good employees or to reduce employment related spending? Each choice has repercussions, as well as a host of systemically related issues that must be considered before the most suitable decision becomes apparent.

2. **Values**—What are your *principles* or standards of behavior?
   Sometimes decisions are difficult to make because they go against your values and principles. If you believe people are the most important part of your business, you will resist when someone is forcing you to make a decision that minimizes their value. If you place a high value on trust, you will refrain from decisions that destroy the trust you've built with other key stakeholders.

3. **Feelings**—What *emotions* are related to the choices in front of you? Write down each emotion, along with an explanation of why you feel that way. Decisions that elicit negative emotions are often more complex, but this exercise may help isolate the specific aspects of what makes that assessment difficult. Similarly, you'll want to retain the aspects of the decision that elicit your most positive emotions. Your gut instincts will manifest here as well. While more difficult to pinpoint, and initially almost impossible to reason out, learning to recognize and trust your gut will help you to identify when issues exist that may not be immediately obvious or logical.

Over time, you will find your best decisions lie at the intersection of your *priorities*, *values*, and *feelings*. The more experience you gain making complex and tough decisions, the better your ability will be to make them, and the more valuable your leadership becomes to others.

4. SAYING NO
Managing Your Time in a Hyperconnected World

"The difference between successful people and really successful people is that really successful people say no to almost everything."

—WARREN BUFFETT, INVESTOR, PHILANTHROPIST
AND CEO OF BERKSHIRE HATHAWAY

There's a saying that states, "With great power comes great responsibility." Successful people often find this to be true. As their visibility expands and accomplishments increase, they receive many more requests for help and support from others. Leaders with broadening roles are asked to deliver results, and at the same time connect with numerous people inside and outside their organization. And no matter how great their desire to comply, leaders find they're unable to be responsive to the needs they used to easily fulfill in the past. While they *want* to spend time investing in others, they're faced with the challenge of prioritizing the return on the time they spend with each person.

In today's hyperconnected world, leaders also receive more and more requests for connection via various forms of social media. People are continually asking for just 15 minutes of their time to discuss an urgent topic. Meanwhile, in the office, they're encouraged to support employee engagement by increasing their interactions with team members at all levels of the organization. But they only have time to make the connections which will be most productive in accomplishing their professional and personal objectives.

Evaluating Time Requests

As a leader, how can you effectively evaluate the myriad of requests? And how do you say "no" to those impacting your time? Consider the following factors:

- **Goals and objectives**

  Focus on the results you're seeking as part of your work. Will the proposed conversation support accomplishing any of these items?

- **Values**

  Ensure you've identified what's meaningful in the way you live and work. These are the standards of behavior that drive your decisions and ensure alignment with your goals. For example, if you value developing deeper business relationships with your direct team members, you may wish to limit time spent with individuals who are not on your team.

- **Priorities**

  Identify the most critical tasks you must complete to support your goals and remain in line with your values.

- **People**

  Clearly identify the target audience you must reach and impact directly, and who they, in turn, will impact. Ensure your time with them will be multiplied, as they influence others.

173

- **Expertise**
  You'll receive many requests that will lead you off course. Stick to the things you know you do well. If the requests don't align with enough of these factors, you simply have to say "no."

How to Say "No"

We all want to be liked to some degree. We want to help others and minimize negative feedback. But the more we focus on our goals, the more frequently we have to say "no." How can we do this tactfully?

1. *Let others know you see the benefit of their initiative.*
   In this way, you communicate an underlying value that all great ideas have a home, even when those ideas need more refinement and evaluation. But you don't have to welcome all of those ideas into *your* home.

2. **Suggest another option or person who might better serve the purpose.**
   For example, someone approached me for advice about starting a business versus purchasing a franchise. After a few minutes of discussion, it was clear this individual had not explored the pros and cons of either option, nor did he have a specific product or service about which he was passionate. I suggested he contact several organizations that provide classes for budding entrepreneurs to learn more about the process. For me to be of better value to him, he needed to have a concrete idea and well thought out business plan to discuss.

3. **Clarify your values and priorities, and make others aware of them.**
   This could include letting others know: a.) you only take meetings on topics that align with your expertise and interests; b.) you have another key commitment during the time they've requested; or c.) to ensure maximum impact, you focus on speaking at certain types of events.

4. **Be honest, authentic, and kind.**

    A number of people have helped me get to where I am today by providing valuable advice. They did so without expecting anything in return, and I too want to "pay it forward." I may not have time for a 30-minute meeting, but sometimes I can spend 10 minutes of focused time "on the run" to point others in the right direction.

5. **Try an alternate approach.**

    When multiple people request time on your calendar on similar topics, host a group meeting and invite them all to discuss the common theme.

Keep in mind that well-intentioned people will often want to meet with *you* when their issues would be better served by someone else. And they may best benefit from an individual who provides a basic or intermediate level of learning on a topic before they can fully understand the advanced expertise you provide.

Saying "no" is not about *not* being nice. It's about ensuring your time is focused on work that supports reaching *your* goals. Saying "no" enables you to avoid energy draining activities and unnecessary stress. It permits you to accomplish your purpose, align with your values, and focus on connecting with the right people to be of even greater service.

5. LEADING IN A "NO WAKE ZONE"
Managing the Pace of Change

"It doesn't matter how slow you go
as long as you do not stop."

—CONFUCIUS, CHINESE TEACHER, EDITOR, POLITICIAN, AND PHILOSOPHER

I magine that you've just joined a new organization or department, or have been appointed to lead a significant, new project. You're excited about your new role and have been given a charge by your leader regarding specific outcomes and metrics to achieve. After taking some time to evaluate the challenge ahead and get to know the team, you're ready for some "quick wins." There are obvious areas where improvement will impact organizational metrics favorably. Yet as you continue to interact with your colleagues and team members to introduce your plans, their responses are muted. They don't seem to appreciate the value of these initiatives. You continue to meet with key people one-on-one to gain their support and probe for issues, but you keep hitting a wall filled with excuses, pushback, and noncommitment. What's wrong? You've entered a "no wake zone."

What Is a "No Wake Zone"?

Lakes and rivers have "no wake zones" where motorized watercraft are required to operate at low speeds—just enough to steer and make headway, without creating any waves or turbulence in the water behind them. These zones exist to prevent shoreline erosion, protect aquatic life, and keep boats docked nearby from rocking too much. While this space is a small part of the overall surface of the water, it's a crucial area. This is the passageway watercraft must traverse to gain access to the open water. Failing to exercise due caution within the norms of the environment could violate the rules and result in associated consequences.

The Rules for Navigating in a "No Wake Zone"

When you get behind the wheel of a speedboat, you automatically want to go as fast as reasonably possible, for the fun of it as well as to get to your desired destination. The same happens with leadership. You clearly see opportunities for improvement. You try to correctly assess your options for accomplishing them and move quickly toward those goals. That is, until you recognize that the lip service your colleagues gave to reaching organizational goals doesn't match their actions to support your plans to get there.

While your desire is to move faster, the environment is slowing you down. You begin to recognize that the subtle but effective measures in place to protect the existing culture also protect it from the changes necessary to make progress. Any attempts to move faster in bringing about change ruffles feathers and is met with overt and covert resistance. Your only choice is to move so slowly that change is almost imperceptible to you and others. This forces you to learn to progress smoothly at the correct pace, without being perceived as destructive. To do this, you must focus on three areas:

1. **Protect the shoreline.**

    These are the cultural boundaries that represent shared beliefs and values. You must frame the mission, purpose, and scope of your projects in the context of the current culture.

177

2. **Respect the aquatic life.**

   These are people who comprise the fabric of the organization. You must value and leverage their skills and capabilities, and help them to understand how they can best contribute to the future success of the organization.

3. **Beware of the boats.**

   These are the other leaders in the organization, all trying to move their own initiatives forward as fast as *they* can. To move forward, you must manage conflicts, ensure alignment and prioritization, and support common goals and metrics.

In this process, it's important to understand the proper timing the importance of the culture, people, and leadership norms in moving strategies and, therefore, the organization forward. Otherwise, frustration and impatience will flare up (like gunning the speedboat motor) and result in run-ins with the environment.

Making Progress in a "No Wake Zone"

How does this advance the objectives you've been instructed to accomplish? How do you create a positive impact for your customers and provide benefits to stakeholders? And how do you leverage the reservoir of capabilities that you bring to the table? Learning the unique characteristics of the organization and demonstrating a respect for its future direction will help you develop relationships that smooth the pathway for faster change and improvement. You'll then reach open water, where you can move faster with fewer barriers to progress.

As a new leader, you obviously desire quick wins. You see opportunities for improvement and want to move forward to meet clearly identified needs. But by slowing your pace in a "no wake zone," you will learn how to move forward in a manner that demonstrates appreciation for and builds relationships with your environment.

6. ESTABLISHING YOUR TONE AT THE TOP
The Three Cs

"Nearly all men can stand adversity. But if you want to test a man's character, give him power."

—ABRAHAM LINCOLN, 16ᵀᴴ PRESIDENT
OF THE UNITED STATES OF AMERICA

M ichael left the office early for once. He was on his way home to celebrate the position he had just accepted at a new company. After 25 years of hard work and great personal sacrifice, he finally got the vice president position he felt he deserved. He had more than enough experience to step into the role and produce solid wins for his new employer. Everything was moving along smoothly until that night, when he got a call from the executive recruiter. There was a problem with the background check; the search firm couldn't find any record of Michael having completed his MBA. Michael recognized that fact when he presented his credentials. Although he neglected to mention he was two classes short of graduation, he felt his vast experience more than made up for his lack of an MBA. Unfortunately for Michael, his new employer disagreed. The offer was withdrawn, not because he lacked the degree, but because he hadn't come clean about it.

Joan was celebrating for a different reason. Her team exceeded its stretch sales targets for the fiscal year, a herculean effort on the part of everyone. Her leadership, strategic planning, and ability to pull the group together to find innovative approaches to problems had paid off. This news would be well received by investors and provide her and the team with a significant bonus opportunity. The company president called and asked her to stop by his office. As she walked down the hall to see him, she imagined his congratulatory words. She might even get a promotion! But when she opened the door and saw a somber look on his face, with the HR vp already present, she knew the message was going to be very different. Someone had reported a few irregularities in Joan's sales tactics. She had simply taken a bit of interpretive license in several guidelines, a gray area she felt didn't hurt anyone. But the president didn't see it as a minor issue. And he dismissed Joan on the spot for her lack of integrity.

What Happened?

Both executives violated the core values that defined acceptable behavior in their organizations. And those core values are the fundamental underpinnings of establishing and maintaining a certain *tone at the top*. The senior leaders were held to particularly high standards because they were expected to be the role models for how team members should act in a variety of situations.

There are many articles that talk about building a culture of innovation or collaboration in workplaces. They talk about the characteristics of making a company a great place to work. But there are a few critical elements that make the place fit for work. They are the 3 Cs, the basic ingredients of establishing each organization's tone at the top. Just as flour is a basic ingredient in baking a cake, and a power source is a basic ingredient in a vehicle, *character, civility,* and *commitment* are the basic ingredients for establishing the tone at the top of a company.

1. Character

Character encompasses a person's mental and moral qualities that lead to their behaviors. A representation of their ethical traits, character governs how they treat others, how they handle adversity, their measure of integrity, what motivates them, and what they do when no one is looking. Some leaders hire for capability over character. I recommend hiring for character over capability. Many capabilities can be learned and improved. But character goes to the core of the candidate's values and is harder to change. Individuals with character flaws may be able to mask them for a while by complying with accepted behavioral norms, but sooner or later, as they're faced with situations and choices, coupled with increasing power in the company, those flaws will be revealed.

2. Civility

Social media and the 24/7 news cycles have had an unfortunate effect on what used to be respectful discussions. They amplify disagreements by providing an accessible platform for dissenting opinions, and enable instant feedback on every bit of information available. People engaging in public and free speech have become more uninhibited in using hateful, negative, and critical tones with one another. While we must understand and recognize the variety of opinions that exist, in order for organizations to function we must learn to disagree agreeably. That means respecting others' rights to have varying points of view. It also means that where possible we should find areas of shared agreement, and explore the reasons behind our differences to achieve workable solutions. Life is full of compromises that require understanding and respect. The ability to listen to one another and to engage in civil discussion around diverse perspectives is a critical element for individuals to grow and develop as a team. Civility can also support team growth towards innovating new solutions and performing at a higher level.

3. Commitment

A key responsibility of leadership is demonstrating a commitment to compliance with external laws, regulations, and policies governing their business, and putting proper internal controls in place to ensure fulfillment and transparency. More than just paying lip service or going through the motions, leadership must ensure employees understand this as part of the embedded values of the organization. Violating such controls may be illegal, immoral, unethical, or simply unwise. And while there are obviously some gray areas of interpretation, intent and actions are key factors.

One impactful way to communicate the range of acceptable behaviors is through using the power of storytelling, where leaders provide examples of how they want employees to behave. Effective leaders also use impromptu settings and situations to speak to employees about the organization's commitment to "doing the right thing." They make it clear to their teams they prefer to hear the "bad news" of the business, rather than implying that employees should take steps to inappropriately "fix or fake" things to create an acceptable report. While some leaders may not overtly take a negative action, they set a tone with their team that it's OK to "stretch the truth" or "interpret the law or rule differently" to achieve the desired outcome.

Set the Tone

This *tone at the top* starts with the board, the CEO, and the senior leadership team. They establish the environment and hold themselves and others accountable. They identify leadership competencies that align with the desired behaviors and evaluate performance against those competencies. Their position on these matters must be visible and their behavior transparent. Double standards, a disproportionate need to justify decisions, and displaying behaviors that require excessive explaining are all red flags that must be addressed.

Sometimes, establishing and maintaining the tone at the top requires tough decisions, like negatively impacting an otherwise high-performing leader. Or public admission that the quality of your product or service isn't up to par. Or publicly addressing a behavioral issue that a predecessor failed to deal with effectively. But doing so makes a bold statement, one that becomes imprinted on the team as a positive example of the leader's and organization's values.

In March 2019, public indictments were issued against wealthy U.S. CEOs and media personalities as part of a scheme to get their children into the "right" universities. Within days these individuals stepped down (voluntarily or involuntarily) from leadership roles in their companies or were dropped from their TV contracts. The organizations' leaders recognized that their behaviors didn't set the correct tone at the top, and given the public nature of the accusations (they are still innocent until proven guilty in a court of law), it was an unnecessary distraction both internally and externally.

This is why it's important for leaders to engage in consistent evaluation of their business practices to ensure they're setting the right tone at the top of their organization.

7. YOUR PAIN POINT
The Motivation for Change

"Change happens when the pain of staying the same is greater than the pain of change."

—TONY ROBBINS, AUTHOR, LIFE COACH, PHILANTHROPIST

I had a conversation with several leaders recently about changes they needed to make in their organizations. They *said* that they wanted to change, but their behavior did not align with that statement. After further discussion, it became apparent that for them, the *perceived* pain they would experience to change their present situation was greater than the *actual* pain of continuing in it, even with an impending negative impact for others involved.

They aren't alone. For many people in similar situations, there are enabling factors that create barriers to change. In some cases, their present situation may feed needs for status, power, attention, or increased financial rewards, even as it creates other problems.

Sometimes there are others who benefit from the constancy of the negative situation, and change would disappoint or disadvantage them in some way. These enablers perpetuate an environment that makes it seemingly vital to continue the ineffective, unproductive, and emotionally dishonest behavior.

What Drives Your Pain?

Pain points are driven by a variety of situations. Here are some examples:

■ Working in positions or a career area you no longer enjoy or aren't very skilled at because of the social status or financial gains it provides;

■ Exhibiting unprofessional or emotionally unintelligent behavior because it makes you feel powerful or helps to accomplish self-centered goals;

■ Maintaining outdated and ineffective people policies that fail to engage and retain employees because you're unsure of what culture change will look like;

■ Avoiding cost reduction measures in the midst of falling revenues because of a reluctance to restrict spending or shift strategy;

■ Delaying difficult business decisions or reorganizations, because they may reflect negatively on your leadership and legacy;

■ Avoiding addressing a team member's unproductive and disruptive performance because you value their historical business knowledge or technical skills;

■ Complacency with the status quo, because the effort to drive change requires more intellectual and emotional energy than you can muster up.

You recognize the pain because it manifests in worry, loss of sleep, physical symptoms, erratic behavior, poor decisions, negative environmental cues, and increasingly becoming out of touch with what your inner spirit is telling you to do. In essence, you're emotionally running from the truth and denying the facts that surround you. You'll eventually find that the actions you take to try to sustain your current course become increasingly ineffective. You may experience periods of *denial* that the situation isn't working out, inappropriately *blaming* others for outcomes, or expressing *anger* at others for seemingly unreasonable expectations.

The interesting part of such challenges is that the longer you delay, the more people in your environment become aware of the need for change. Stakeholders demand results, employees become disengaged, and teams spread negative reviews of your leadership. Ultimately, a delay in facing your pain point harms not just you, but your entire organization.

Your Tipping Point

Even when we *know* that we should change our behavior, real change often doesn't occur until the pain of our present situation is greater than the pain associated with change. This is our tipping point, and we need to embrace the fact that it's coming. As you think about where you are uncomfortable with your current situation, start by asking one key question:

What is the risk of change versus staying the same?

Pull out a sheet of paper and write your long-term goal on the top. Below that, on the left side, list the likely outcomes if the current situation continues, including the ways it harms you, other stakeholders, and the organization. Then, on the right side, write down what you think change would look like, along with its associated benefits. Yes, this is a simplistic start, but it is a beginning to envisioning a more productive future *before* you reach the point of immense pain.

In medicine, physicians prescribe pain pills to be taken *before* you experience significant discomfort. The goal is to get ahead of the pain before it becomes overpowering, and therefore more difficult to treat. Similarly, better decision-making occurs when you're not operating from a place of emotional or intellectual pain, or in reactionary mode. Here are four pain pills you can take to motivate yourself to embrace change:

- Be **proactive.**
  Make decisions when your thoughts are clear and the pressure isn't on you to sacrifice quality for speed.

- Be **uncomfortable.**
  This comes with growth and stretching. If the work is easy, you're not driving enough improvement, so press forward.

- Be **focused.**
  Like glittering pebbles by the roadside, there will always be many distractions. Prioritize your objectives and keep your eye on the goal.

- Be **disciplined.**
  Take daily actions towards your goal. Yes, it's hard, but the longer you delay, the more painful the change will appear.

All change begins with the first step. Start by identifying *your* pain point and how you will change.

8. WHAT TO DO WHEN YOU DON'T HAVE A DREAM TEAM
Scrambling

"Teamwork is the ability to work together toward a common vision. The ability to direct individual accomplishments toward organizational objectives. It is the fuel that allows common people to attain uncommon results."

—ANDREW CARNEGIE, BUSINESSMAN AND PHILANTHROPIST

L eaders spend a great deal of time focusing on building strong teams, selecting the right people with critical skill sets, managing diversity of thought, and matching complementary strengths. They structure their organizations based on the capabilities needed to accomplish objectives and optimize opportunities to control as many variables as possible to ensure a cohesive team.

But what happens when you don't get to pick your dream team? What happens when you're assigned to work with a group of people and must determine how to best come together to accomplish a goal? This frequently occurs when you're part of a team with a shorter lifespan, sporadic interaction, or representing diverse and distant stakeholders. Thus, the ability to craft the membership and spend time in team building is reduced. For example, you may be:

■ **Assigned to a one-off project**
You may be a subject matter expert appointed to work together with other subject matter experts to solve a complex problem. In this case, members are identified solely based on their area of expertise.

■ **Part of a volunteer group**
You have a common passion for the task at hand, but you come together infrequently or for a brief period.

■ **Managing through a crisis**
When a quality, health, or safety incident occurs, it's "all hands on deck" to quickly address and resolve it.

■ **Evaluating a situation**
This includes sitting on a jury, judging a Shark Tank-like presentation, or preparing a group assessment of others' performances.

■ **A community-wide coalition**
Influential leaders of diverse and separate organizations often come together to address a common problem that will benefit their respective constituencies regarding economic, social, health, or education issues.

Scrambling to Adapt

In these situations, you may be forced to adapt to a team where everyone learns each others' strengths and weak points to accomplish the task at hand as you simultaneously work on a project.

Consider this scenario. I was playing in a golf scramble and found myself part of a foursome for a nonprofit's annual fundraising initiative. In full transparency, our group included my husband paired with his weekly golfing buddy, and my cousin paired with me, the latter very sporadic golfers. As a group, the depth of our relationships varied from distant to intimate, and we had never golfed all together. Our only pressure to excel was self-inflicted by our competitive natures. Yet ultimately, the learning was not so much about golf but about operating as a team. In particular, a team that must form, storm, norm, and perform all within a brief period of time to achieve a goal. Under pressure to complete our round in four and a half hours, we moved swiftly through that process.

- **Form**—We <u>assessed</u> our teammates' *capabilities* and *interests*. The four of us spent the first three holes learning each others' strengths and adjusting to differences in styles. Some of us were dealing with the frustration of not providing the value we wanted to the team and trying to improve our alternately poor shots.

- **Storm**—We <u>asserted</u> our own *capabilities* and *interests*. When the "best ball" shot wasn't obvious, the more experienced golfers (two guys) took the lead in determining which ball to play. Us less experienced golfers (two ladies) felt we had to go along with them because we couldn't depend on our shots to get us out of trouble. But we weren't always happy about it. Yes, we grumbled in our cart and schemed about how we would gain the upper hand. Oh, and did I mention that the guys weren't interested in looking for our cute, lost balls?

- **Norm**—We <u>appreciated</u> each other's *capabilities* and *interests*. As we warmed up to the course and settled in, we learned when we could count on one another to make certain shots. We began to strategize as a team on how to optimize shots on each hole. And we ladies began to insist on using a few of our "best balls."

- **Perform**—We <u>maximized</u> each other's *capabilities* and *interests*. Finally, we began shooting par. A birdie even popped up here and there! We felt confident in our strokes and moved smoothly around the course. Our scores also improved for each hole.

Lessons We Learned Along the Way

1. **Use the strengths of each member.**
   When you're baking a loaf of bread, you'll normally use a lot of flour. But without the smallest ingredients, like a little bit of yeast, your loaf won't rise. A surprisingly small strength, like someone who serves as a relationship connector between members, may turn out to be the glue that holds the team together.

2. **Provide and accept encouragement and support.**
   With your new team, you must decide to exhibit mutual respect for each other, even when you don't agree with all the perspectives and can't yet appreciate the varying skill sets. Be open to the learning that may take place as you interact with and support one another.

3. **Assert value to the team.**
   When you feel a key asset is being overlooked, whether yours or someone else's, first understand the motivations of others in the context of the goal. Then present the value of that asset in a manner that aligns with the motivation and goal.

4. **Protect what's important to you.**

Given we were playing a difficult course, we lost more balls than normal. That was fine, until we ladies lost a ball we really liked, and realized the guys weren't as concerned about looking for those lost balls as we were. It was a minor issue, but meaningful to us, so we stopped using our favorites in risky situations. Don't offer something you value if others aren't yet ready to value it.

5. **Align your gift with the team's needs.**

Teams may have more than one member with a specific talent. The abundance of that talent could be an advantage, or to fill a void, one individual may instead need to focus on using a different skill set that no one else on the team demonstrates.

Having a *dream team* is a wonderful aspiration, but there will be many situations where that's just not possible. Instead, you'll have to adjust your approach to fit the circumstances and people assigned to you. Be self aware of how your behaviors contribute to building the team, and how to maximize others' talents and personal styles to reach your goals. In the midst of it all, you can find a way to accomplish your goals.

9. SUSTAINABLE LEADERSHIP
What Happens When the Glue Fails?

*"Leaders don't create followers,
they create more leaders."*

—TOM PETERS, AUTHOR, BUSINESS
MANAGEMENT EXPERT

A key requirement of good leadership is to ensure that the organization and its initiatives are sustainable, both during and beyond the leader's tenure there. This means the company's values, beliefs, goals, and objectives cannot be dependent upon a single person, or a few people, as the glue holding it together. Situations will inevitably occur where such individuals are no longer a part of the organization, and thus the glue fails.

Frequently, business start-ups and transformations are initially driven by individuals who possess the personal characteristics necessary to bring a team together and drive toward a goal. But they must always transfer those qualities to others to sustain the growth of the business. They must multiply themselves throughout the organization to ensure that the right people are in place to maintain and carry it forward.

The Glue

The "glue" leader in an organization typically exhibits the *vision* to see future possibilities, a *passion* or personal resolve to pursue an otherwise unattainable goal, and the *capability* to accomplish it. There are several well-known examples of CEO-founders who were the glue for their company's success. When they left those roles, the "glue" failed, and their companies struggled until they returned to provide strong guidance that resulted in improved business outcomes.

Steve Jobs

Cofounder of Apple, Jobs left the company in 1985 after a disagreement on product strategy. The company went through a series of CEOs and failed products before Jobs returned and was appointed CEO in 1997.

Howard Schultz

Schultz became CEO of Starbucks in 1982, growing it from four to over 3,500 stores with $2 billion in revenue. He resigned in 2000, but returned eight years later because performance was declining and he felt the organization had strayed from its core values.

Michael Dell

Dell founded Dell Computers as a freshman in his college dorm room. He grew it from 1984 to 2004, when he moved away from daily operations yet remained chairman. But three years later he returned to the CEO role to address declining sales.

The same principle applies when two pieces of steel are welded (glued) together as part of assembling a vehicle. The welding forms a series of bonds along the length of the pieces, establishing a continuous connection between them. If one weld fails, it won't separate the whole. But if there aren't enough welds, no matter how strong each one is, the bond between the two pieces will be fragile and susceptible to breakage.

The Ingredients

As a leader, you can build an organization that is sustainable not only while you're there, but as a legacy when you depart. Here are several keys to developing sustainability:

- **Practice humility.**
  Never believe you're the only one capable of providing such leadership. Instead, believe you're the right person for the right time, and bring others into your circle of leadership.

- **Plan succession.**
  By coaching, mentoring, and developing others in your area of expertise, you will ensure the future capability of the organization.

- **Actively communicate.**
  The vision can't be fully contained in your mind; you must repeatedly share it with others in your organization, enabling them to "see" it and understand their role in accomplishing it. They must be empowered to pick up the mantle, take it as their own, and share it with others.

- **Build culture.**
  There are beliefs, values, behaviors, and processes that support an engaging company culture. These must be identified, practiced, and improved upon to ensure repeatability.

- **Encourage innovation.**
  Encouraging your team to bring new ideas and approaches to achieving business goals is a must. This includes challenging well-established assumptions, and exploring different possibilities for what the future of your organization's products and services may look like.

Leadership is a team sport; many players working together, playing their roles to win. This is what supports an organization and creates a legacy for the future. Build a sustainable team of leaders.

10. LIFE INTERRUPTING WORK
But It's All Life

*"You will never be satisfied by work
until you're satisfied by life."*

—HEATHER SCHUCK, ENTREPRENEUR AND AUTHOR

For most leaders who are results oriented, high powered, and fast paced, life *is* work. But what happens when life *interrupts* work? Consider the following scenarios.

In February 2018, one of my best and oldest friends passed away. I was so glad I had the privilege of spending the last few days of her life with her. I cancelled my role in leading a meeting and rushed to the airport in tears to catch an earlier flight than I originally had planned in order to be with her. It was precious time that I wouldn't trade for anything. But it impacted me more than I realized. Several weeks later, I realized there were some work-related items that had totally slipped my mind while I was supporting my friend's family and processing my grief.

In mid-2017, I was facilitating a meeting of women business owners and casually stated that I wasn't at an earlier meeting because...then I suddenly burst into tears...sobbing! Fortunately, I was in a "safe space" where those around me were very supportive, though confused by my unexpected behavior. After a few minutes, I finally was able to communicate that thinking about missing their earlier meeting triggered the memory of being with my husband, who was undergoing a heart transplant at the time. And my emotions came pouring out uncontrollably.

Some years ago, the son of a gentleman who used to work for me passed away at age 20 from a tragic cancer diagnosis. Family, friends, and coworkers gathered for two and a half hours at their church to celebrate his life, during which time none of us dared to breathe deeply lest we break down crying. Afterwards, we were all so emotionally exhausted that one business unit leader cancelled his strategy planning meeting scheduled for later that day. And I was of absolutely no value in the meeting I *had* to attend that afternoon.

And these are just the situations I remember!

Work-Life Balance

What happened? Life interrupted work. In the midst of deadlines, pressure, politics, production planning, and performance, the *personal* aspect of life became a priority. I could no longer put on my stoic and composed face and focus on the tasks at hand. I was reminded, again, that it's all about people and relationships. Because without people, the products and services we provide mean nothing. As leaders, we must understand and address our people needs above all else.

Here are my "AHAs" through this journey:

- **In the never-ending search for work-life balance, there's a tipping point where you can literally fall over.**
  There's simply too much "stuff" on either side of the scale. It's important to recognize when you're becoming too off-balance, and find a support system to steady yourself.

- **Don't overestimate your capability to manage in times of intense stress.**
  Just because you can't see what's going on doesn't mean others aren't seeing it.

- **Emotional health, like physical and mental health, should be a priority.**
  Even though you may not have a formal or long-term diagnosis doesn't mean it isn't an issue. Find an outlet to release the stress.

- **Asking for help isn't a sign of weakness, it's a sign of wisdom.**
  Often people want to help you, but don't know how, so give them a chance to show you they care.

Finding that right work-life balance is different for everyone. Sheryl Sandberg, COO of Facebook, says there's work, there's life, but there's no balance. Others say it's not a balance but a blur. I believe that it's all *life*, and we simply have to prioritize everything based on what's most important at the moment. Minimizing a family emergency to attend a work-related meeting may not be the wisest choice, if you're unable to focus on the discussion. Similarly, ignoring an urgent email from your boss on the weekend may not be the wisest decision. Manage the demands on your time by communicating with everyone involved, and ensure they understand what you're working on and when you expect to deliver it. And let each person know you value your relationship with them.

LEADERSHIP BEHAVIORS REFLECTIONS

Hopefully, you felt challenged by this group of articles. Maybe you found a need to reevaluate your own behaviors and underlying values, and make some adjustments going forward? Ensure you're sending the right messages and backing up your words with the right actions. Here are some further reflections on **Leadership Behaviors**:

◆ Who are you really serving in the organization and how are you meeting their needs?

◆ How can you ask the right questions to support quality decision-making?

◆ Where do you need to resist the pressure to make a premature decision on a project?

◆ Where do you need to rearrange your priorities and simply say "no" to some requests?

◆ Where are you struggling to make change happen fast enough and how do you need to modify your approach?

◆ What "tone" are you setting for your team? What examples do you want them to follow?

◆ What is driving pain in your life, and what is the risk of change versus staying the same?

◆ How can you shift your expectations of the members of a short-term team to maximize results?

◆ Are you building success strategies and processes that can be sustained if and when you leave the organization?

◆ How do you need to realign your priorities to ensure that you plan your time appropriately?

By now, these ideas should be making an impact in your approach to leadership.

Step 6.

Essential elements for accomplishing your leadership goals

T he next group of articles covers **Leadership Tools,** the essentials
needed for accomplishing leadership goals. These concrete
elements enable you to enhance your leadership effectiveness. From
this vantage point, you can fill your "toolbox" with the most important
techniques, tips, and strategies to gain your desired results. While
there are many such elements that will support your leadership, these
articles describe those which are particularly meaningful.

1. ILLUSION OR REALITY?
7 Fundamentals to Being a Realistic Leader

*"People don't want to hear the truth because
they don't want their illusions destroyed."*

—FRIEDRICH NIETZSCHE, GERMAN PHILOSOPHER,
COMPOSER, CULTURAL CRITIC, AND POET

I recently watched a video of the famous illusionist David Copperfield making the Statue of Liberty vanish in front of a group of spectators. The statue weighs 450,000 pounds and stands 305 feet tall, so moving it is not an easy task. To accomplish this trick, Copperfield set up a special stage where the viewing audience would be seated to witness his performance in the dark of night. The stage was framed in front by pillars, which held a curtain secured at ground level that could be raised or lowered to block their view of the statue. Also at ground level, a circle of lights illuminated the stage, and the statue's presence was tracked on a radar screen visible to all.

Copperfield presented the statue to the audience, then raised the curtain for a few moments, blocking their view. When the curtain dropped again, search lights beamed through the spot where the statue once stood, showing nothing was there. It had vanished, leaving only the ground-level lights to mark its footprint! After raising the curtain again for a few moments, Copperfield then dropped it to reveal the statue, back in place.

How did he do it? During the time the curtain was raised, the audience viewing platform and pillars rotated slowly to the right, so that when the curtain dropped, the statue was behind a pillar. Music was blaring throughout the show to distract the spectators, and the radar display was fake.

Copperfield's spectacular show, performed in 1983, was full of entertainment and flair. The audience was amazed, even in the midst of the fact that the sculpture couldn't simply disappear. They couldn't figure out how it was done, thus they bought into the reality of the illusion. That feat was listed in the book of *Guinness World Records* 2014 as the largest disappearance ever performed by a magician.

Illusions

We're often spectators to other illusions in our world that are not necessarily executed by traditional magicians. Such illusions may be manifested in the form of major initiatives taken on by leaders and their teams to accomplish admirable goals, but fail to address other related organizational problems hiding in plain sight.

When these illusions involve addressing significant business challenges (like statues weighing 450,000 pounds), they are not easily or quickly resolved. For example, innovative new technologies need to be thoroughly tested and validated, with sufficient training and communication provided to users to ensure consistent results. A business strategy, merger, or acquisition may promise great gain, yet the realities of the market or economy may negatively impact the ability to accomplish it. And when leaders are promoted because they're intellectually or technically competent, but everyone knows their leadership capability or emotional intelligence is not sufficiently developed to lead their team, the organization's performance will suffer.

Illusions can admittedly be more pleasant and soothing to the conscious mind, however, they are temporal. While they draw our focus from the truth of the challenges we face, ultimately, we must address those challenges.

The Reality

Conversely, realistic leaders establish a solid foundation from which they and their team can construct sound solutions. Here are seven fundamentals for becoming a realistic leader:

1. Be **transparent** in your communications with stakeholders to establish an environment of trust. While it's necessary to maintain appropriate confidentiality, your work can't be so secret that no one fully understands what's going on.

2. Be **truthful** about the current facts and challenges of the business. Accept bad news in the same way that you embrace good news.

3. Be **open** to ideas, feedback, and information from others on possible solutions. Encourage your teams to collaborate and share data, even if that material differs from your current strategy.

4. Be **strategic** and take the time to research and analyze the proper decisions and actions to ensure success. Be willing to take responsible risks.

5. Be **pragmatic** and address issues sensibly, based on what's actually happening, without over relying on unproven theory. Look for practical options and evaluate each one carefully.

6. Be **optimistic** and think positively about the future and the potential to win. Communicate a compelling vision of what *can* be and build momentum toward achieving it.

7. Be **performance** based so that your results speak louder than your persona. Recognize the importance of your behavior to drive needed change and model proper ethics. Leverage your strengths and surround yourself with others who possess complementary capabilities.

Being realistic does not mean accepting mediocrity or minimizing grand plans for the future. It does mean clearly acknowledging the present challenges that must be addressed to support those future plans. Realistic leaders dream of ambitious possibilities, but then they get to work understanding the problems and issues in the present and develop a pathway forward. They are not seduced by illusions of grandeur but are influenced by thoughtful opportunities.

Be a realistic leader.

2. CRACKED CONCRETE
Is Your Business Foundation Sound?

*"Because if you have a strong foundation like
we have, then you can build or rebuild
anything on it. But if you've got a weak
foundation, you can't build anything."*

—JACK SCALIA, ACTOR

Not long ago, my husband and I realized that we would soon have
to repair or replace the circular concrete driveway in front of
our home. We thought it would last a lot longer. Instead, after only
14 years, several concrete slabs are sinking; weeds are creeping up
in the spaces between them; a large crack is running through one
slab, courtesy of a heavy delivery truck; another slab is scaling; and
the snow plows that are a staple of Michigan winters have left scrape
marks on other parts.

We never thought this would happen because those concrete
slabs *looked* so strong and thick. We could wait another year or two,
but the situation will only get worse. What we thought was a solid
foundation with high structural integrity wasn't resilient enough to
withstand a variety of above and below ground pressures. What if the
quality or thickness of the concrete had been stronger? What if we

had ensured that heavy vehicles didn't pull into the driveway? What if we had carefully used a walking snowplow each winter, instead of hiring a heavy truck to plow it? In hindsight, it was hard to predict we'd be in this spot, but we now needed to look at options to repair or replace all or a part of the driveway.

A Fortune 500 Foundation

Leaders, employees, and investors in certain Fortune 500 companies, who thought their positions in these companies were sound, inevitably realized there was a problem. Over time, companies that were an annual fixture on the Fortune 500 list fell off when profits shrunk precipitously, and other companies struggled to find new footing. Obviously, all companies face similar challenges, but the question is how well they withstand them. One can't assume that just because a company has been top performing, well regarded, or high revenue producing, it will always remain in that position. There are a host of so-called blue-chip companies that have gone through bankruptcy, been sold or split, or even ceased to exist. In fact, only 61 of the companies on the Fortune 500 list in 1955 were still on the list in 2014. That means 88 percent are gone.

I'm sure many of the leaders and investors in the 1955 list thought the foundation of their companies was strong enough to last forever, and couldn't have fully anticipated the internal and external forces that would come against them. But they discovered their structural integrity was insufficient, their foundation was sinking.

How Sound Is Your Foundation?

A sound business foundation starts with people. Leaders must possess the capabilities, capacity, values, and cultural competencies to fulfill the organization's vision, mission, and objectives. They must understand competitive and market pressures, and correctly anticipate future events. The reality though, is that even the largest businesses, with the highest revenues and the best leaders, are subject to become like that cracked cement. So how do you prepare for the inevitable? Here are four steps to make sure your foundation is sound:

1. **Recognize**

   Watch for signs of stress and pressure, not only as evidenced by your business metrics, but the small, faint cracks that indicate a weakness in your strategy or approach. Ensure your company culture reinforces the importance of people calling attention to any weakness to force a spotlight on the issue.

2. **Plan**

   There's a saying that a building is only as strong as its foundation. I used to work on the top floor of a 39-story, glass building. On extremely windy days, you could feel the building swaying, however, it was built to withstand and bend with high winds. Occasionally, a glass panel in the elevator shaft would break, but it was always quickly replaced. In the same way, ensure your business planning and contingency process has a solid foundation to withstand extreme forces, and a strategy to quickly adapt and adjust to changing conditions.

3. **Act**

   Be decisive and resolute in taking action to address cracks when they show up. This is where you may have to make hard and unpopular decisions. An unrepaired crack on your vehicle windshield will only spread, and an unaddressed problem will only become magnified, sometimes very quickly. What appears small on the surface may really be a huge issue below the surface and require more resources to address later.

4. **Reinvent**

   Be adaptable to restructure, reengineer, or reinvent your business to address shifting market demands. HP and Xerox both split into two companies to meet changing market demands that their leaders may have never anticipated five or 10 years ago.

   Just like cracked concrete, your crumbling foundation can be repaired or replaced. It may look different than it did before, but it will be better positioned to withstand the future changing business environment.

3. MANAGING YOUR VUCA
4 Keys to Thriving in an Unpredictable World

"VUCA flipped: Velocity, Unorthodoxy,
Co-creation, Abundance"

—GERD LEONHARD, EUROPEAN FUTURIST AND HUMANIST

When *Fortune* magazine publishes its annual list of the largest U.S. corporations, the names are all familiar. Only about 5 percent of the companies are newcomers. But understanding the challenges some of these companies have faced over the past years tells a clearer story of the shifting headwinds. One popular acronym used today is VUCA, which stands for Volatility, Uncertainty, Complexity, and Ambiguity. According to writers Nathan Bennett and G. James Lemoine in the January-February 2014 issue of the *Harvard Business Review* ("What VUCA Really Means for You"), your level of VUCA reflects how much you know about your situation and how well you can predict the results of your actions.[29]

Other articles and books are being published that similarly reflect the increasing pace and scale of change in our environment, along with the need for leaders to become comfortable with *discomfort.* C-suite leaders who finally win the brass ring can no longer rest on their laurels, nor can they clearly forecast the next major trend. Instead, as the saying goes, they are now an easier target for competitors and detractors. More frequently these days, their appointment comes on the heels of their predecessor's perceived shortcomings and/or the mandate to reinvent their companies and themselves.

Even the best leaders are scrambling to keep pace, much less outrun their competition. In early 2014, on Doug McMillon's first official day in his new position as Walmart's CEO, he found it difficult to actually sit in the chair in what used to be Sam Walton's office. Whether he was momentarily overwhelmed by the magnitude of running the Fortune 1 company or by the admired history of its founder, it took a moment for McMillon to mentally and physically make the shift. For a company under competitive pressure from the likes of Amazon and dollar store chains, his leadership is critical to pushing through the challenges ahead.[30]

As McMillon and other leaders press forward to maximize the success of their companies, several tips come to mind that are critical for everyone to follow to effectively manage their VUCA.

Dance on the Balls of Your Feet

During my career, I've observed many executives who I've placed in the category of needing to "learn how to dance." In other words, they needed to learn how to flow with suddenly changing business situations and lead by coming up with new solutions quickly. *Dancing on the balls of your feet* takes this to the next level. In the dance world, as in the business world, doing so is a function of your quickness, balance, movement, and smoothness; all necessary traits for managing VUCA. Your leadership style, organizational culture, and decisions must be agile to smoothly and swiftly pivot the company's strategies and direction when competitive threats loom, and to take advantage of new opportunities when they arise.

Wear Your Trifocals

Unfortunately, I've reached the age in life where trifocals are a necessity. At the bottom, I have the strongest prescription so that I can read and see things close up. I use the middle area to focus on objects and words at midrange, like my computer screen. And at the top, I can see far into the distance. Though I don't wear them 100 percent of the time, I admit that my vision isn't as precise as when I have them on. Fighting the need to wear them only places me in denial.

So what is your strategy for seeing things in your business up close, midrange, and far into the future? Indra Nooyi, former chairman and CEO of PepsiCo, saw that while her company makes a lot of money on what many consider to be junk food, consumers really want more healthy fare. To address that, she led the long-term stategy to continue optimizing the current big moneymakers while developing new products that taste good, but without the unhealthy ingredients.[31]

Use Your Shoe as a Cell Phone Holder

You rightfully should think that this sounds crazy. But 25 years ago most people had not heard of a smartphone, Apple watch, Facebook, or many other staples of our modern age. This is innovation, which means combining multiple objects that have no obvious relationship with one another to create something new and different. Innovation is a matter of changing your mental perspective, shifting your view of how things should operate, and meeting needs that people didn't realize they had.

Play a MMORPG

For the uninitiated like myself, MMORPG is a Massively Multiplayer Online Role Playing Game in which a very large number of players interact with one another within a web browser based game world. With tens of millions of players and revenues worth tens of billions of dollars, this category is continuing to explode.[32] The theme is to create and develop a character in an online fantasy world where the culture, systems, and environment continue to evolve, even when you're not playing it.

While this gaming world may seem totally unrelated to organizational strategies, the founders at Improbable, a London start-up, have taken it to a new level. According to *Forbes*, the company has created new technology to "simulate extremely complex systems."[33] Bossa Studios, another gaming company, is using Improbable's technology to create a new MMORPG, and organizations like Samsung and Oxford University are using it to run simulations and future scenarios. These organizations are trying to understand the impact of volatile, uncertain, complex, and ambiguous events on the future, without having to actually wait for them to happen. So game theory can help you model and manage your future.

Obviously, organizations and leaders who learn how to manage effectively in a world of increasing unpredictability are the ones with the best shot at reaching their goals. They will be more perceptive than lucky, anticipating change even when they're unable to understand it. They will thrive where others merely survive, fueling themselves on the pace of change rather than drowning in it. They will shift their perspective on VUCA, viewing it as an opportunity rather than an obstruction.

29. Nathan Bennett and G. James Lemoine, "What VUCA Really Means for You," *Harvard Business Review*, January-February 2014, https://hbr.org/2014/01/what-vuca-really-means-for-you.

30. Brian O'Keefe, "he Man Who's Reinventing Walmart," *Fortune*, June 4, 2015, http://fortune.com/2015/06/04/walmart-ceo-doug-mcmillion/.

31. Jennifer Reingold, "PepsiCo's CEO Was Right. Now What?" *Fortune*, June 5, 2015, http://fortune.com/2015/06/05/pepsico-ceoindra-nooyi/.

32. Christina Gough, "MMO and MOBA Games Market Revenue Worldwide 2017-2021," *Statista*, May 15, 2018, https://www.statista.com/statistics/830090/mmo-moba-market-revenue/.

33. Parmy Olson, "Meet Improbable, The Startup Building the World's Most Powerful Simulations," *Forbes*, May 27, 2015, http://www.forbes.com/sites/parmyolson/2015/05/27/improbable-startup-simulations/.

4. PROBLEM SOLVING
6 Steps to Collaboration

"We cannot solve our problems with the same thinking we used when we created them."

—ALBERT EINSTEIN, GERMAN MATHEMATICIAN, PHYSICIST, AND NOBEL PRIZE WINNER WHO DEVELOPED THE THEORY OF RELATIVITY

Many years ago, when I began my career in human resources, a colleague gave me a piece of valuable advice. He told me that when providing HR expertise and support to other business leaders in the organization, I should avoid being a "no" person. Instead, I should find ways to say "yes."

Now, you must understand the context of this conversation. There were times when these business leaders would make what I call "end" requests. That means, when they identified what they perceived to be an HR related problem, they would decide what action needed to be taken and tell us in HR how to resolve it. The relationship was supposed to be a mutual balance of influence, and where appropriate, in compliance with policies, so neither of us could fully direct the other on what to do. You could assume these leaders jumped to their conclusion because they anticipated a recommendation from us that they didn't like, and in some cases you would be correct. However, in our humble yet expert opinions, their solution wasn't the appropriate way to resolve the issue because it often didn't take into account all the considerations to be managed in addressing it.

These leaders weren't necessarily trying to be difficult or violate policies or procedures, they simply wanted a quick resolution that met their needs. As HR professionals, the temptation for us, at least periodically, was to take charge of the situation and resolve it in the way we thought was best. But the better result always included myself and my colleagues collaborating with the leaders in understanding how to assess the problem and in finding the best solution for the company, the team, and individuals involved.

Supporting Consistent Growth

Professionals from all areas of expertise face similar challenges in resolving conflicting perspectives and priorities regarding business problems, particularly in rapidly expanding or shifting organizations. The need to achieve consistency and alignment in policies, processes, and procedures increases with the complexity of the industry and the business strategies. For early stage organizations, the "do whatever it takes to get the job done," "create it as you go," or "break all the rules" attitudes must necessarily evolve into more uniform and disciplined approaches to business. In all organizations, leaders and team members must know the underlying values, the behaviors expected of them, and the appropriate steps to address a variety of challenges. Staff members must be adept at understanding the needs of their partners in order to collaboratively resolve problems in creative ways, thus balancing a variety of needs.

Take Constructive Steps

So how do you best collaborate constructively with business colleagues to solve problems, particularly when their "end" request is far from the proper way to address the situation? How do you simultaneously strengthen relationships, demonstrate empathy, and uncover creative approaches? Often, the pressure is considerable to take a specific action within a short timeframe, but such decisions are better served by thoughtful responses. Here are the recommended steps to guide you.

1. **Acknowledge** the request.
   Let your business partners know you heard them and that you're committed to helping them.

2. **Understand** and get to the underlying need.
   Ask questions and do your research to ensure that you fully understand the issue. Ask the 5 Whys, or this list of Ws.

   What is the desired result?
   Who are the stakeholders?
   What are the short-term and long-term goals?
   What are the enablers and the roadblocks?
   What is best for the organization as a whole?

   Then take a break. Literally. Step away from the intensity of the conversation to provide careful space to consider what's next.

3. **Reframe** the issue.
   Based on your responses to the questions in step 2, restate the underlying issue that the leader is trying to address. For example, instead of pushing back on hiring a specific candidate, selecting a particular supplier, or eliminating a business expense, talk about your common business or project goals and criteria for success. Then discuss how the request aligns with those goals.

4. **Identify** the relevant cultural behaviors and norms that should align with the result.
   Effective CEOs should establish and communicate these behaviors and norms within their organizations, and the role of their leadership team is to model them whenever possible.

5. **Find** common ground.
   State the areas of mutual agreement. Emphasize that you're on the same team.

6. **Get** to "yes."
   Instead of saying "no," state what you will do to address the concern. Identify the benefits of your proposed solution. Give your business colleagues options where possible. Clarify the drawbacks of any options that would conflict with laws, legislation, compliance, internal policies, values and behaviors, employee relations, etc. Show how your proposed solution will contribute to meeting their overall business needs.

Offer Win-Win Solutions

There are obvious benefits to these six steps to collaborative problem-solving. They include:

- Understanding priorities in different areas of the business
- Increasing engagement and appreciation of colleagues' expertise
- Practicing innovative strategies to resolve business problems

We found that when our business colleagues understood we would value their point of view while pursuing win-win solutions, they brought us fewer ready-made answers. Instead, they proactively discussed their concerns with us and we worked collaboratively to develop the best solutions for everyone involved. We learned to value and respect each other's expertise to support business growth.

5. LEARNING IN ACTION
7 Facilitation Strategies for Leaders

"We cannot teach another person directly; we can only facilitate his learning."

—CARL ROGERS, FOUNDER OF THE HUMANISTIC APPROACH TO PSYCHOLOGY

Along your leadership journey you will increasingly find yourself at the front of the room. You'll likely be standing there with the goal of influencing anywhere from five to 5,000 people in a particular course of action, sharing corporate policy decisions, facilitating a learning experience, discussing business challenges, developing and integrating business plans, and more. You'll be faced with managing external compliance goals, internal policy decisions, varying leadership opinions, and diverging employee preferences. Your objective will be to broaden the perspective of the audience and gain consensus around a set of values, strategies, and actions.

Walking into the room solely focused on *your* agenda is a recipe for disaster, as it will result in your audience feeling that you don't care about their concerns. You must anticipate every aspect of the topic, environment, and attendees to properly prepare for and address your subject matter. Your approach may be interactive and participatory or more formal and direct. But building a relationship with your audience is always critical for success. As a leader, part of your growth involves understanding how to facilitate others' learning experiences to accomplish organizational objectives. In the process, it's essential for you to be open to continuous learning from those around you as well.

A Culture That Encourages Learning

How do you encourage learning and growth in your organization? Here are 7 key strategies to consider as you leverage your leadership skills!

1. **Plan the environment.**
   This seems basic, but it's often taken for granted. Think about what you want to accomplish and ensure the environment is designed to support that. For instance, if you want the group to envision the future, don't hold the meeting in an interior room with no windows. Instead, find a space they don't normally meet in with an expansive view. One of my most inspiring settings for such a meeting was in a 26th floor conference room with floor to ceiling glass on a clear day. Similarly, if you want participants to interact with and learn from one another, arrange the seating in small groups, rather than rows of chairs facing the front. If you want to inspire creative thinking, ensure a stimulating and colorful environment.

2. **Build rapport with the participants.**
   Begin your interactions with attendees when they enter the room, not when the meeting begins. If you haven't had a chance to meet them yet, this is a great time to connect with them and find areas of common interests. If you already know them, this is the time to reinforce those relationships. Throughout the meeting, interject comments linking you to the participants and acknowledging their interests and concerns. This reinforces engagement and underscores your support of them. If your discussion requires convincing participants about a specific plan of action, spend time *before* the meeting talking individually with the "influencers" to

219

listen to their concerns and ensure they understand the issue. Know everyone's position on the topic *before* the meeting so that you can appropriately address each one.

3. **Choose your battles.**

Invariably, if your topic is controversial, you're going to prepare for a spirited discussion. Begin with the points that most participants can agree on to build momentum before moving to the more provocative areas. If you know the group wants to be critical and change your outcome, include a less significant issue where you're willing to acquiesce. In some situations, rather than propose a specific course of action, lead the group to recognize a general need. Then they may ask you to take an action you already know is vital. And stay in tune with the mood of the room, so you'll know when to press forward on an issue or when to pause and come back to it later.

4. **Deflect an argument.**

With a provocative topic, someone will invariably ask a challenging question. To avoid a heated debate in the room, try responding with a clarifying question, like "Help me understand why that's important to you" or "Help me understand what you mean by that." You may find you have greater areas of agreement than you thought. Follow up on points of contention *after* the meeting. And focus on what you *can* do, not what you *can't*.

5. **Learn to dance.**

Good dancers know how to fluidly respond to whatever type of music is playing. Similarly, develop your ability to respond in the moment to whatever is happening. This means you'll have in-depth knowledge of your subject matter and will focus on the body language and comments from those in the room. If you see that your participants are not responding to the presentation as planned, shift your style, your examples, your visuals, and your learning approach to meet their needs. After all, it's about them, not you.

6. **Be authentic and genuine.**
We've all had moments when we watched a skilled facilitator or presenter with awe, wishing we could deliver in a similar fashion. But the best we can do is to find our own genuine superpower and be the best version of ourselves. Our body language will telegraph if we're nervous, so we must be comfortable with the message we're communicating. Acknowledge difficult points where necessary and be as transparent as possible. Leaders who stand before a group of employees to deliver an unpopular message must display empathy and sincerity; implying that a such a message has positive value to employees will quickly erode trust and respect.

7. **Reengage your audience.**
Sometimes, as meetings flow, the facilitator recognizes that a portion of the group has become distracted or disengaged. Recognize this quickly and pull people back into the discussion by telling a relevant and great story to make a point. You can also change the pace and pitch of your speaking to create a shift in the room and draw others out of a momentary lull. Or call out the name of one or two people to involve them in the discussion or find a way to make people move (drop something on the floor!). Finally, you might mention the person's behavior. "Jane, you appear concerned, do you have a particular question?"

Remember, as you're building your facilitating skills, don't run from being uncomfortable. Like muscle building, growth occurs in these awkward spaces, and you learn to bring others along with you in the learning process.

6. YES...#METOO
6 Options for Empowerment

"Never accept anything less than you deserve.
Remember, you teach people how to treat you."

—UNKNOWN

Metoo. That's the refrain from a number of my female (and some male) colleagues and friends who reluctantly admit a time when they were the target of unwanted and inappropriate attention from someone. These are accomplished, influential people who found themselves in a situation where a more powerful person demanded undeserved, intimate fulfillment.

The demands may have come by way of improper or sexually themed text messages, a "gentle" but suggestive touch on the arm, a lewd remark at a bar, an expectation to continue a business conversation over drinks and dinner, an out-of- town meeting scheduled in a hotel suite where everyone else suddenly leaves the room, and the list goes on. The common denominator is a situationally more powerful person assuming the right to gain personal gratification from a less powerful person. The aggressor tries to take advantage of the victim's desire to:

- Get or keep a job or a promotion
- Sign a deal or gain a new customer
- Secure investment dollars
- Benefit from their influence and favor
- Accomplish an important project or build valuable relationships

No matter our roles or responsibilities, we may still find ourselves in a position where we have to be clear in advance about what we're *not* willing to do to accomplish those goals.

Anger, shame, fear, and anxiety are but a few of the emotions that flood our minds once we find ourselves in these situations. We rehearse how we might have handled these circumstances better or differently. We want to take action to regain our power, but have to consider the consequences of that as well. Will we be believed or blamed? Often, there's no "proof" or witnesses, or no one to tell who *can* or *will* hold that person accountable. At other times we worry that addressing the perpetrator can create ongoing, negative consequences for us.

While discussion of these topics is now more open than ever, and we see many public examples of companies dismissing or firing leaders who have engaged in such conduct, the waters are still murky. When confronted with accusations of misbehavior, organizations tend to weigh policies and values against the loss of key leaders, negative stakeholder reactions, and financial repercussions. Yet business-to-business relationships are at risk, based on employees stepping up to report inappropriate behavior that often has been going on for years.

Take Back Your Power

We appreciate those individuals who continue the dialogue, bringing the issue of inappropriate workplace conduct to the forefront of our consciousness. This puts pressure on leaders in positions of power to properly create and sustain a climate where this behavior is not tolerated. But we also have to manage day to day and interact with individuals who say, #IDidntDoThat, as in "You misunderstood my actions" or "You'll never do anything about it." While there is no perfect answer, here are a few options:

1. **Decide where you draw your lines.**
    I know of some prominent men who won't have dinner alone with another woman or won't be alone in a room with a woman. It may sound extreme, and some worry it inhibits men from mentoring women, but that's the lengths they'll take to avoid the specter of poor behavior, a wrong accusation, or misperception. When an unfamiliar or unreferred male contacts me and requests a meeting, I typically start with a conference call to screen him. If he won't agree to that, he doesn't get a meeting.

2. **Phone a friend.**
    If you're unsure about an upcoming event or situation, call a trusted friend to discuss the setting and attendees to get a second opinion. Sometimes our focus on taking care of business and accomplishing a goal blinds us to the subtleties of an environment or agenda. One of my colleagues will phone a friend during a meeting, clearly stating where she is, what she's doing, and when she'll be leaving. Her intention is to ensure that a questionable person in the room will know that others are tracking her whereabouts.

3. **Use your intuition.**
    Many years ago, I worked with a leader who I suspected was the type to engage in inappropriate workplace relationships. He was friendly with me, and at times three or four of us leaders would have lunch together. One day I was standing in my office talking to two other people when I saw him out of the corner of my eye. He came down the hall towards us with a smirk on his face and his eyes locked on me. As he got closer, he didn't break his stride or eye contact. I instinctively stretched out my arm, palm facing him, to stop him. And I gave him my "Are you crazy?!" look. If I hadn't done that, I felt he was going to kiss me or get REALLY close to

it. As I'm recalling the scenario, it sounds absolutely ridiculous. The perpetrator knew he was wrong. And he never behaved inappropriately with me thereafter. Trust your instinct about certain people and adopt protective behaviors to minimize your chances of being harassed.

4. **Control the environment.**
You can probably control more of the environment than you think. If you're meeting with someone you don't have good vibes about, bring a colleague or arrange for a person to "happen to stop by" at an opportune moment. Or you can select the meeting location or time and involve others in the conversation. There have been instances when I've created a reason for rescheduling or relocating a meeting because I didn't feel comfortable with the arrangements.

5. **Be willing to walk away.**
This is the hard part. I believe I'm just as capable as any man of performing my job, and I don't like to feel I need to approach situations differently or be left out because of my gender. But there are some meetings I've decided not to attend because I don't feel comfortable in the environment (i.e., a lot of men and booze) or with the personalities (i.e., arrogant and oblivious to others' opinions). Maybe I missed a good business opportunity. Maybe I didn't. I'll never know, but I had to make a tough decision in my own best interests.

6. **Bravely speak up.**
In many of the now public harassment allegations that have come to light over the past several years, where multiple recipients were involved, many people knew that "John" had an issue, yet no one addressed it. There's strength in numbers, but it takes one person to start a movement. You could start by asking, "Is it just me or is anyone else uncomfortable with this situation?" Document your experience. Share it via available reporting venues. Then review option 5 above.

Respect

One of the earliest records of unwanted affection is in the Bible, when Potipher's wife pulled Joseph's clothes off as he ran away from her repeated advances. She then lied about it to her husband, accusing Joseph of making a pass at her. It's been going on for thousands of years, so regrettably, I expect these issues will never disappear. But I hope all of us will feel more empowered to address them.

Remember, you won't always be able to prove that the other party's negative behaviors occurred. You won't always like how the situation is handled. You might sue, and after a lengthy process win some money, but money shouldn't be your motivation. You want respect, empowerment, justice possibly. So review your options and decide what you need to do in order to regain that empowerment and respect for your professional capabilities.

LEADERSHIP TOOLS REFLECTIONS

You've just learned some very practical tools to improve your leadership effectiveness. When they are overlooked, there's a negative impact on business processes and outcomes. Conversely, paying close attention to them will enable you to connect with the core components to connect with your team, identify and manage problems, and ensure your plans have a solid foundation.

Here are further reflections on **Leadership Tools**:

◆ Where are you creating an illusion of success, instead of a realistic view of a business challenge?

◆ How strong is the foundation of your business, or is there a crack running through it?

◆ What's the effect of VUCA on your work and how are you managing that?

◆ What problems are you trying to solve and how can you take a different approach?

◆ How can you improve your facilitation skills?

◆ How can you promote an environment where inappropriate behavior is clearly defined and not tolerated?

Hopefully, you now have concrete steps to take to augment your leadership. Start by prioritizing those items that will have the biggest impact. You will also likely find that taking action in one area will easily impact outcomes in a related area and provide a compound improvement.

Step 7.

LEADERSHIP
IDEAS

Wisdom for pursuing goals

T he last group of articles, **Leadership Ideas,** provides wisdom as you pursue your goals. From this vantage point, leaders drive concepts forward. Yet it's necessary to have a realistic assessment of the context in which they will be successful. As you read about these ideas, you may initially think that the learnings are for more entrepreneurial leaders. But consider the intrapreneurial competencies that your company wants to develop in its leaders. Think of the importance of how you connect your professional passions and ideas with your work. That's what makes these essential.

1. YOUR DREAM OR YOUR NIGHTMARE?
Keys to Successful Small Business Development

"You are not your résumé, you are your work."

—SETH GODIN, AUTHOR, AND ENTREPRENEUR

This is supposed to be your dream come true. Finally, your business is up and running. You're breathing life into your big idea. No longer do you have to answer to the boss because you *are* the boss. You're working your business plan and finding your path to financial freedom. You know your target market and you're gaining new clients. With positive feedback on your current products and services, you're developing new technology. You're securing additional funding. You've finally found the right team to work with and have the right workspace. You can feel the exciting energy when you walk into your business each morning.

Yes, there are bumps in the road, but you're learning to be resourceful and move through, over, or around them. Each day is long and brings surprising new trials, yet you're gaining momentum, along with new customers and increased revenue. You learn to balance the ups and downs of the market and business challenges. You learn to pace yourself. However, as time passes and you analyze your business growth, you see that the trend line isn't moving upward, it's declining. Your plans aren't working out as you expected. At this rate, you're not sure how long you can continue operating. You realize that as passionate as you are about the business, the problems are overwhelming you. Your dream is turning into a nightmare!

Why Small Businesses Fail

In spite of your best efforts, your business is succumbing to one of the top 10 reasons why businesses fail (nonprioritized list, according to Jay Goltz, *The New York Times*, January 5, 2011).

1. Owners who cannot get out of their own way
2. Operational inefficiencies
3. Dysfunctional management
4. The lack of a succession plan
5. The math just doesn't work
6. Out-of-control growth
7. Poor accounting
8. Lack of a cash cushion
9. Operational mediocrity
10. A declining market

The first four reasons in particular are linked to how you develop and lead your business. Small business owners who seek expert advice in running their business have a better shot at overcoming these pitfalls. To address them, here are nine tips for successful small business development that are critical components for you as a small business owner.

1. **Be a learning leader.**

Be purposeful about leading and designing your company for success. If you think you know everything necessary, and close your mind to new and different ideas, you AND your business will stop growing. Instead, find a business mentor, attend workshops, read books, keep a bias for learning, and set the example for your team.

2. **Manage your passion.**

Don't let your passion manage you. Just because you love shoes doesn't mean you should open a shoe store. Make sure you've identified the void in the marketplace that your business can fill, or the need that you're satisfying. Make sure you know your target market and understand what they're willing to pay and do for your product or service. Then assess your financial resources. There are too many stories of entrepreneurs who had what seemed to be a great idea, got over their heads into debt, and then tumbled into bankruptcy.

3. **Increase business value.**

Your greatest business value resides in a combination of your people, processes, products/services, technology, and customer relationships. You must understand exactly where the value resides and how you best provide that value to others. Then preserve and improve upon it. For instance, guaranteeing same-day service and thorough cleanup by your technicians could be your greatest value. But to provide such a service, you must have a sufficient number of trained technicians on call at all times and a reliable 24/7 contact and communication process.

4. **Build your culture.**

This is the DNA of your business. Whenever a client comes in contact with your business, whether face-to-face, by phone, by email, or by social media, they gain nuances and impressions that determine whether they want to continue to engage with you. Set the tone by treating your employees the way you want them to treat your customers. Make customer service a priority. Create a welcoming and comfortable environment. Ensure the style or décor will appeal to your target market and effectively represent your product or service.

233

5. **Position your family.**

Do you have a *family business* or a *business family*? Does your business exist as a place to employ your family or a place to serve your clients? The wonderful family members who helped you get started may need to evolve into different supporting roles as the business grows, ensuring you have the most qualified people in positions where they can perform well.

6. **Develop your successor.**

Your role in founding your business is important, but none of us are irreplaceable. Constantly develop others to learn the business, and make leadership decisions based on what will add value to the company. Your business legacy is only valuable if you invest in its future and anticipate that one day you will need to pass the leadership mantle on to someone who can take it farther than you. This person may make different decisions based on a different competitive environment and available resources.

7. **Understand business roles.**

Roles and responsibilities must shift as the business grows and/or the market shifts. Be flexible, clarify responsibilities, and ensure accountability.

8. **Document business processes.**

Continually review and update your operating processes to maximize efficiencies. Involve the employees who actually perform the task and find ways to eliminate waste, rework, and scrap because they all result in lost revenue.

9. **Build support networks.**

Many entrepreneurs and business leaders have forged a path ahead of you. They've failed, made mistakes, learned, and persevered. They have expertise that will be valuable to you. Make those connections when you're in the early planning stages of your business and continue to develop them as you grow. Gaining professional help in all phases of strategic planning for your business will result in greater expertise to ensure your success.

Becoming a small business owner is a lot like falling in love. Once you fall madly in love with a seemingly fantastic person, it's more difficult to recognize your areas of incompatibility. Similarly, once you have what appears to be a fantastic business idea you're passionate about, it's more difficult to see the potential pitfalls to your success. So take time now to carefully plan the strategies and criteria for your business success.

2. PASSION
Blinded or Balanced?

"Follow your heart, but check it with your head."

—STEVE JOBS, COFOUNDER, FORMER
CHAIRMAN AND CEO OF APPLE

Ann Marie Sastry had a big idea. With over 70 patents and 80 scientific publications to her credit, she described herself as a "happy warrior who's driven by doing the next, new thing." That drive led her to put in 100-hour workweeks and spend over two decades in pursuit of developing new battery technology for use in electric vehicles. She scrapped the traditional chemical lithium technology to rethink the basics of energy, power, mass, volume, cost, and safety in search of a new approach. She also raised $30 million from a variety of backers in support of her grand idea.[34]

Sastry's entrepreneurial zeal for her product compelled her to pursue any and every approach and perspective to accomplish her goal. Her passion and optimism for success propelled her forward, ensuring her product would be in full production. But for every successful entrepreneur, there are multiples more whose dreams never turn into reality. The same passion that propelled Sastry forward with a clear focus on success can be blinding to others, causing them, unfortunately, to miss obvious cues indicating their grand idea won't get off the ground.

An article in *The Wall Street Journal* by Noam Wasserman, entitled "How an Entrepreneur's Zeal Can Destroy a Startup," provided perspective on the negative effects of such passion.[35] It's displayed in the many mistakes founders make in starting their business, which include a lack of technical or scientific experience, management experience, and connections with investors and potential customers. New entrepreneurs significantly underestimate the time and resources needed to get the business running, and the toll it will take on their family relationships.

Interestingly, one study showed that when 800 founders' startup ideas were assessed and given feedback on the feasibility and next steps of their business, of those who received a recommendation that their ideas weren't commercially viable, 29 percent continued to invest money and 51 percent continued to invest time in development. The obvious question at this point is why someone would continue to pursue a venture when they're highly unlikely to succeed. The authors suggest that these individuals had overwhelming optimism in their potential for success, coupled with a reluctance to give up after already investing so much time and money. In short, they were blinded by their passion.

Founders are often driven by a desire to make a mark in their world. They may believe their idea will play an important role in their environment or society, and they feel compelled to pursue it. Their passion becomes the focal point of their thought process as they move forward to accomplish their dream. Passion managed appropriately can have a positive impact, while unchecked and unbalanced passion may lead to negative behaviors and consequences. Passion for an initiative can open one's eyes to new possibilities, yet it can blind one to the potential difficulties of pursuing it. Passion can drive entrepreneurs to sacrifice the presumed comfort of a steady paycheck to pursue their business startups, but it can put their finances, family, and future at risk.

Thus, too much of a good thing can become a bad thing. So, how do know if your passion is out of balance? Ask yourself the following questions:

Do you have the emotional support of your family?
Or are you sacrificing too much time to pursue your passion? Many entrepreneurs fail to be honest with themselves and their loved ones about the commitment required to pursue their dream.

Do you have the financial resources to support your business idea?
Do you have sufficient finances for your personal living expenses? Are you draining your retirement savings? How are you funding this venture, and how much are you willing to invest and borrow to determine if it has a chance of success?

Will your business help build positive relationships?
Or do your friends and colleagues avoid you because this is the only thing you talk about? Engaging in conversations on a variety of topics with individuals from various backgrounds can serve as a creative catalyst, versus being singularly focused on your project.

Do you have the skill set to accomplish your dream business?
Or are you able to gather others around you with the right talent to support your efforts? Too many entrepreneurs try to do it all, when in reality they need to surround themselves with people who possess a variety of skill sets that will evolve over time.

Does your business idea meet a need, fill a void, or satisfy a desire in the marketplace?
Are people really willing to invest in it or pay for it? What may seem like a wonderful idea to you may lack sufficient value to others.

If you responded "no" to any of these primary questions, this is the time to think carefully about what you're doing. This is the time to make sure your zeal is not overshadowing reality and focus on initiatives where you *can* be successful, where you *can* fulfill your responsibilities to family and friends, and where your talents *can* be most valued.

This isn't suggesting that you give up on your passion. Instead, refocus and apply it where it will be most beneficial. Whether your passion is an entrepreneurial venture, a great new idea for a process or product within your organization, a pastime, a hobby, or a business initiative, balance is the key.

34. Brian Dumaine, "Will This Battery Change Everything?," *Fortune*, September 18, 2014, http://fortune.com/2014/09/18/sakti3-lithium-ion-battery/.

35. Noam Wasserman, "How an Entrepreneur's Passion Can Destroy a Startup," *The Wall Street Journal*, August 25, 2014, http://online.wsj.com/articles/how-an-entrepreneur-s-passion-can-destroy-a-start-up-1408912044.

3. IDEATION SPACE
Your Most Productive Moments

"Ideas can be life-changing. Sometimes all you need to open the door is just one more good idea."

—JIM ROHN, ENTREPRENEUR, AUTHOR,
AND MOTIVATIONAL SPEAKER

I *deation space:* the optimal environment where you form ideas or thoughts, where dreams crystallize, desires are birthed, problems are solved, and creativity blossoms; a place where your senses are heightened as you connect deeply with your inner motivations and interests, and block out external distractions. Purposefully spending time in this space requires disconnecting from the daily demands of the *urgent* and *immediate*, and connecting with the *important* and *meaningful*. It involves moving from the emotions of the moment to reflecting on the underlying values and beliefs that govern your life. Time spent in your ideation space can rejuvenate you to become more productive, focused, and innovative.

But what you do *after* you've spent time in your ideation space makes all the difference. Do you move forward, carefully clutching the thoughts produced during that time like they are priceless pearls to be inlaid in a majestic setting, or the inspiration for Michelangelo's painting in the Sistine Chapel? Or are your warm thoughts quickly dampened by reality, as if hit by a cold blast of Arctic air? You must protect the ideas and insights you've gained and look for the opportunity to apply them, test them, and turn them into reality. You must take action as a result of your time in your ideation space.

Ideation Leaders

The ideation space for Max Levchin (cofounder of PayPal) is his company named HVF Labs, short for Hard Valuable Fun. He considers it the intellectual outlet for all the ideas that pop up in his brain. His team focuses on leveraging data collected through low-cost sensors, wireless broadband, and advances in distributed computing and storage to develop value-added applications. One of their products is an app called Glow, which crunches and analyzes vast quantities of data to provide information and insights about women's bodies, offering the optimal timing for conception and enabling them to make appropriate decisions about their reproductive health.[36]

Marc Benioff, CEO and founder of Salesforce.com, is energized by being around customers and other creative people. They stimulate his thinking and get him to ask the right questions. Benioff believes the quality of his questions on a topic directly correlate to the quality of his innovation. Like Andy Grove, he concludes "only the paranoid survive," and is thus constantly considering inventions for the future, even if it means ditching something he's started and beginning anew.[37]

Ideation Teams

Like individuals, teams also need an ideation space. This is where they become more productive, think outside the box, and find new ways to solve old problems by innovating and challenging the status quo. Visionary leaders ensure that they provide the right environment for ideation, prioritize time for the team to engage in this practice, and take action on the outputs. This means creating the right setting for collaboration on projects or casual discussions that morph into creative brainstorming. The aesthetics of the workspace, use of color, furniture style, textures, lighting, and exterior view all play a key role. So does the ability to capture and find the connections between ideas, issues, and problems. Sometimes it will involve creating a lab to model or diagram new concepts, and at other times it's just getting the team out of the normal environment and into a different space to spark innovation.

As a leader, how are you creating the right ideation space for your team? How are you providing the right environment for your team to think from a different perspective, to test ideas that may become game changers for your organization? How can you set the stage for them to be more creative and solve problems? Having an ideation space is an investment in your team members as individuals and a collective group. While it could be a "go to" meeting spot, more effectively, it should be part of their daily work atmosphere, so they can integrate the problem-solving process into their normal routine. You also can involve your team in the process of designing their work space, developing their work processes, and seeing their ideas come to life.

Find ways to "reward" new ideas, even if they aren't feasible. That will help get the team into the mode of thinking differently and lay the foundation for coming up with very successful ideas.

And finally, model the behavior you want your team to exhibit. Think about your own optimal ideation space and share what that looks like with the team. Talk about what it takes to stimulate your own thought process and encourage them to do the same. Discuss the benefits of spending time in this environment so everyone understands it is a priority. Then enjoy your space.

36. Preetisha Sen," How Max Levchin's Glow App Got 25,000 Women Pregnant," *Fortune*, August 27, 2014, https://fortune.com/2014/08/27/how-max-levchins-glow-app-got-25000-women-pregnant/.

37. Adam Lashinsky, "Salesforce CEO Marc Benioff on Where Big Tech Is Headed," *Fortune*, January 22, 2015, http://fortune.com/2015/01/22/salesforce-ceo-marc-benioff-on-where-big-tech-is-headed/.

4. THE TENACITY TO WIN
Don't Give Up Before It's Over

"Don't quit. Never give up trying to build the world you can see, even if others can't see it. Listen to your drum and your drum only. It's the one that makes the sweetest sound."

—SIMON SINEK, AUTHOR, MOTIVATIONAL SPEAKER
AND ORGANIZATIONAL CONSULTANT

H *ave you ever worked hard on a project, anticipating the final result, only to see it shift* AT THE VERY END? This was the fate of fans at the Michigan State University (MSU) versus the University of Michigan (U of M) football matchup on October 15, 2017. If you're a graduate of either school, or if you even live anywhere in southeast Michigan, you feel the intensity as game day draws near. Students and employees wear their game colors on the Friday before the big day. Homes and vehicles fly the school flags. Trash talking reaches an all-time high, even for people who don't typically watch college football.

There were over 111,000 fans in The Big House (U of M's stadium) on this Saturday to watch the game. And it was made more intense by the excitement over the start of Jim Harbaugh's new coaching career at the University of Michigan and Coach Mark Dantonio's strong reputation for winning at Michigan State. Sportscasters and other experts offered a myriad of opinions on why either team should or would win. Bets were placed across the country.

U of M held the lead throughout the game, and in the final 1:30 minutes, the score was 23-21 in their favor. Coach Harbaugh let the clock run out by calling safe plays. The University of Michigan fans were rejoicing in the stands and on social media. Meanwhile, the Michigan State fans were trying to manage their disappointment—they had won six of the past seven such games and were in no mood for losing.

After a long day of partying and sitting in the open stands, where temperatures barely rose above 50 degrees, it would have been easy to just leave. Yes, with less than two minutes to go, it was tempting to get a jump on some of the exiting crowd, find a spot to eat dinner, and beat the traffic. The outcome seemed obvious. No one would have complained about giving up and leaving before the game was over, no matter which team you were rooting for.

Well, anyone who did so on that Saturday was in for a rude awakening. In the final 10 seconds, the University of Michigan fumbled a punt and the ball fell into the hands of a Michigan State redshirted freshman safety. He ran like crazy, 38 yards into the end zone, making a touchdown and winning the game 27-23.

The crowd was in shock. Fans of both teams, whether in person or watching on television, collectively said, "Did I just see what I thought I saw?" Those who were jubilant seconds ago were now speechless. Those who were depressed a moment ago dissolved into uncontrollable glee. *And those who left before it was over or turned off the television or radio before the clock ran out didn't have a clue.* In fact, one local TV station did a full minute broadcast announcing U of M as the winner before they learned of the surprise ending!

Both teams fought hard to win. There were close calls, bad calls, mini victories, and plenty of roadblocks along the way. After all, the winning team gives bragging rights to hundreds of thousands of people for a full year. But if you really support your team, your initiative, or program, you have to stick with it until the end. You have to give it every effort, no matter how dark the prospects look. The question is whether you really *believe* you can win.

If that player, Jalen Watts-Jackson (who unfortunately suffered a season-ending hip fracture as he hit the ground in the end zone), hadn't taken his role seriously, even when they were down 2 points with 10 seconds left in the game, he never would have been able to run the ball for the play. If he, or the other Michigan State players had given up on the field, their dream would never have come true.

When have you left the field before the game was over? When have you given up with the end in sight, either because you thought you'd accomplished your goal, or you thought your chances of winning had died? You worked hard on a project, pursued an aspiration, came up with a great idea, or tried to finish an initiative. Maybe things appeared to be going smoothly and you thought you could coast to the finish line, only to find that the last major roadblock was waiting for you there. Or maybe you struggled the entire time, so close but yet so far, until you thought all hope of succeeding was lost. You walked away defeated, not wanting to even hear the death knell.

Think of where we might be today if Thomas Edison had stopped after 999 experiments with the light bulb. Whether you consider this just a game, or the most significant play of the year, it's most importantly a clear example of life lessons.

Even when you think the outcome is clear,
don't give up.

Give it your all, all the time.

Don't leave until it's over; don't give up
before it's over.

It's not over until it's over.

And just for the record, this author is a proud U of M alum.

245

LEADERSHIP IDEAS REFLECTIONS

As you reflect on these **Leadership Ideas**, think of them as the spark of wisdom that will broaden the impact of your leadership. This is a vantage point for expanding on your underlying passions and fueling the innovation and creativity necessary for remaining competitive in your work.

Here are further **Leadership Ideas** for reflection:

◆ What ideas do you have for new company initiatives, and are you approaching them from the perspective of launching a profitable business with the right leadership capabilities?

◆ Does your passion for these initiatives overwhelm the reality of how to ensure their success?

◆ Where do you generate the best ideas for yourself and your team?

◆ How do you ensure you create the right environment for your team to ideate and innovate?

◆ In what areas do you need to work as hard as can until you cross the finish line?

Your responses should provide the stimulus for continued action to accomplish your goals.

CONCLUSION

J eb settled into the booth across from Sue at their usual breakfast spot. He had taken several months to carefully read all of the articles she sent, and during that time gained a whole new outlook on leadership, which transformed him. He always knew his peers at the company admired Sue. But only after learning about her approach to leadership did he fully understand why.

After placing their usual orders, he blurted out, "Sue, if you're so bright, why didn't they appoint you as CEO?"

Sue smiled a bit wistfully, then laughed, "Fifteen years ago, I was on the succession short list to become CEO. I was appointed executive vice president five years earlier, and my career path was all planned out to get me to that role. But along the way, I discovered that I didn't really want the job. I worked close enough to Jack, the CEO at the time, to understand the challenges and responsibilities in his role. And at the end of the day, I realized that I enjoyed my evp role much better. I was closer to the technology and the product. I was able to have greater influence on how we developed and trained our future leaders. I just loved the role I was in. And quite frankly, I also didn't like some of the choices I would have had to make in the CEO role.

"Jack and the board chair spoke with me several times to try to persuade me to change my mind, but I knew it was the right decision for me. It wasn't about money, or prestige, or the added perks. It was about knowing my leadership purpose, and every other decision flowed from that one."

Jeb nodded. After everything he had learned, he now understood the thought that had gone into the decisions Sue made. He knew too many senior leaders who aspired to the CEO role, but he recognized they wouldn't be the best choice. He wondered if they realized it too, but they felt compelled to voice their interest nonetheless as they navigated corporate politics.

Jeb's thoughtfulness shifted to excitement. Several weeks earlier, after a presentation to the executive team, he happened to mention to Curtis, who joined the company as CEO two years prior, what he had been learning from Sue. Curtis seemed genuinely interested and commented that he had heard from others that Jeb seemed to bring a new and more engaging and effective approach to his leadership. Curtis wanted to meet with him and learn more about the change that was occurring. Jeb shared this with Sue, then paused. "I admittedly don't think I'm the best person to discuss this with him," he said to Sue. "Will you come with me to the meeting? I want him to hear firsthand from you what you learned while working at the company."

Sue laughed. She remembered about four years ago when she tried to share her learnings with the prior CEO, Martin, whose tenure was short-lived. At the time, she knew she was about a year from retirement and wanted to "give back" to those coming along behind her. Sue could think of no better way than to share her articles, but Martin wasn't really interested. Two years later, the board replaced him with Curtis in a move to provide stronger leadership to meet customer needs and change the culture.

Jeb went on. "I told Curtis about the work you did while you were with the company. He's heard a lot about you from some of your colleagues and is looking forward to meeting you." Sue smiled. She wasn't sure what the outcome of this discussion would be, but she was very interested in talking with Curtis. Her ongoing contacts with several of her former colleagues kept her abreast of some of their challenges.

Weeks later, Sue settled into the familiarity of the CEO's office. Jeb joined her there, introduced them, and reviewed how he reached out to Sue and how she helped him. He was comfortable with Curtis and talking about his own growth journey. Curtis listened intently as Sue spoke about her learnings in the organization and the articles she compiled. He asked insightful questions, his mind obviously churning. When they finished, Curtis smiled. "This is what I've been looking for," he said. Curtis needed someone with the obvious respect of many of the current leaders, who at the same time could drive the changes he felt were necessary to make an impact in their market. He had interviewed various consultants and candidates for senior roles, but here she was, right in front of him. Without pause, Curtis offered Sue a role back in the company, focused on developing successful leaders. He told her she could pick the terms and create her own schedule.

Jeb beamed and quietly excused himself from the room so they could discuss the details privately. For the first time in a long while, he felt he was really in the right position and company, where his strengths were appreciated and the senior team was invested in his growth. It seemed like Sue had also achieved her dream role. This was the culmination of 40 years of growth for her. Jeb strode back to his office energized by their conversation and his future potential.

ABOUT THE AUTHOR

Priscilla Archangel, Ph.D., has a passion for strengthening leaders, teams, and organizations to clarify and fulfill their purpose, and believes "everything rises and falls on leadership." As an executive coach and a leadership and organizational development consultant, she offers practical solutions for real challenges, along with insightful and candid feedback. Priscilla collaborates with business leaders to develop and implement effective people strategies to support their objectives through leadership development and training, organizational design and development, organizational communications, employee engagement, and talent management. She facilitates learning experiences to promote participant discovery and problem solving.

A John Maxwell Team certified coach, speaker, and teacher, Priscilla delivers keynote and motivational speeches on leadership and organizational development topics to business and professional groups. She engages and captivates her audiences by challenging their perspective, causing them to reflect on their leadership, and calling them to a greater purpose. Her greatest joy is seeing the light in others' eyes as they grasp a concept, gain a new insight, understand a more effective leadership style, and most notably, improve their leadership effectiveness.

Priscilla gained experience in leadership and organizational development during her 30 years at a Fortune 10 company. There, she held a variety of global executive roles and was responsible for leadership development, talent management, talent acquisition, coaching, change management, culture change, performance management, organization development, and HR operations. She was fascinated by understanding behavior and motivation. Her passion evolved as she observed the successes and struggles of leaders with a variety of capabilities, and the impact this had on their teams and organizations.

Besides *LeaderVantage: 7 Essential Steps to Peak Leadership*, Priscilla is the author of *The Call to Faith Centered Leadership: Transformational Lessons for Leaders in Challenging Times*. Her articles have been published in a variety of professional periodicals.

Priscilla was born and raised in Detroit, Michigan. She earned her Bachelor's degree in psychology from Anderson University, followed by her Master's in social work administration from the University of Michigan. She later completed her Ph.D. in human and organizational systems from Fielding Graduate University.

In addition, Priscilla is a licensed minister. She and her husband, Peter, enjoy golf, reading, and team teaching on topics related to marriage and faith.